James George Roche Forlong

Short texts in Faiths and Philosophies

Or Some Sentiments of the Good and Wise

James George Roche Forlong

Short texts in Faiths and Philosophies
Or Some Sentiments of the Good and Wise

ISBN/EAN: 9783337071981

Printed in Europe, USA, Canada, Australia, Japan

Cover: Foto ©Thomas Meinert / pixelio.de

More available books at **www.hansebooks.com**

SHORT TEXTS
IN FAITHS AND PHILOSOPHIES

SHORT TEXTS

IN

FAITHS AND PHILOSOPHIES

OR

SOME SENTIMENTS OF THE GOOD AND WISE

ARRANGED CHRONOLOGICALLY TO SHOW THE MOVEMENTS OF THOUGHT THROUGH THE AGES

BY

MAJOR-GENERAL J. G. R. FORLONG

F.R.S.E., F.R.A.S., M.A.I., Etc., Etc.

AUTHOR OF
"RIVERS OF LIFE" AND "SHORT STUDIES IN THE SCIENCE OF COMPARATIVE RELIGIONS"

PRINTED FOR PRIVATE CIRCULATION
EDINBURGH 1897

TO MY BELOVED WIFE

CONTENTS

	PAGE
INTRODUCTION . . .	9
EGYPTIAN RELIGIOUS THOUGHT . .	15
CHINESE SCRIPTURES PRIOR TO CONFUCIUS	21
JAINISM OR YATI-ISM . . .	25
THE ZOROASTRIAN OR MAZDEAN SCRIPTURES	32
ORPHEANS	36
HINDUISM—VEDAS AND VEDĀNTISM . .	41
HOMER THE IONIAN	48
THALES OF MILETUS . . .	49
ANAXIMANDER	49
LĀO-TSZE, THE FOUNDER OF TĀO-ISM . .	50
PYTHAGORAS, THE WESTERN PUTHU-GURU .	57
THEOGONIS OF MEGARA . . .	60
GŌTAMA "THE BUDDHA," OR SĀKYA THE MUNI	61
BUDDHA'S CREED IN HIS EARLY JAINA STAGE . . .	63
GŌTAMA'S SECOND OR TRUE BUDDHIST STAGE ON LEAVING GAYĀ .	64
PINDAR	73
CONFUCIUS, OR KHUNG-FU-TSZE	73
XENOPHANES	80
HERAKLEITOS, "THE WEEPING PHILOSOPHER" . .	81
'ASKLĒPIOS	82
PARMĒNIDES .	82
ANAXĀGORAS .	83
PERIKLES . .	85
SOPHOKLES .	85
ZENO OF ELEA	85

CONTENTS

	PAGE
EMPÉDOKLĒS	86
PROTAGORAS	87
EURIPIDĒS	88
GORGIAS	89
SOKRATES	90
DEMOKRITOS OF ABDERA	92
ISOKRATES	93
PLATO	94
DIOGENES OF APOLLONIA	97
ARISTOTLE, THE STAGYRITE	98
PYRRHO	100
EPIKUROS	101
ZENŌN OF KITION, THE STOIK	102
KLÉANTHÉS	104
KELTIK OR DRUIDIC TEACHING	105
LUCRETIUS CARUS	107
CICERO	108
HILLEL, JEWISH HIGH PRIEST	109
PHILO JUDÆUS	111
SENECA	113
PERSIUS, ROMAN STOIK AND POET	117
EPICTETUS	117
THE EMPEROR M. AURELIUS ANTONINUS	119
SONTÂLS OF SOUTHERN BANGĀL HILLY TRACTS	121
BODDOS AND DHIMALS OF EASTERN INDIA	122
LEPCHAS, KUCHES AND HÔS OF N.E. INDIA	122
ARAFURAS AND JAKUNS	123
POLYNESIANS, TONGANS, AND ADJACENT ISLANDS	123
AZTEKS, OF OUR MIDDLE AGES	124
PORPHYRIOS	125
MAHAMAD, THE ARABIAN PROPHET	126

SHORT TEXTS
IN FAITHS AND PHILOSOPHIES.

THE great advance of research and discoveries in the science of Comparative Religion and Archæology, makes it advisable to consider how we actually stand in this respect at the close of the XIXth century. We here therefore give a brief chronological epitome of much ancient thought, culled from well-recognised sources: from writings on rocks and stones, mummy cases and cloths; from temple walls, buried tablets, lāts or stēlæ, papyri, bibles and sacred records; and, for clearness and brevity, will throw together the more prominent teachings in the form of free but carefully-translated texts, and in modern language—summarized so as to clearly bring out the leading points of each teacher, sect or school. This ought to enable us to trace the veritable footprints of each and all, as they wandered along—often in doubt and darkness—towards a truer conception of the universe, the unknown and unfathomable future.

It will be a passage adown the Rivers of Life or progress, which ought to show ethnographically, as well as sectionally, the part which each race and nation has borne in the struggle upwards to light and learning; as well as those obstructing influences which have retarded the march of truth by superstitions, self-interests, heredity, or other circumstances peculiar to race, time and climate.

We must not expect consistency in the old speakers or writers any more than among modern ones: one sentiment may often contradict another, and this may be more apparent than real, from our condensing perhaps a chapter of learned and abtruse matter into a few lines. As far as possible it is desirable to actually quote important texts, apothegms or maxims, which thus taken alone, perhaps occasionally too strongly accentuate the views of the old sages; yet, excepting this unavoidable treatment, which the reader can allow for, the rendering will be strictly in accordance with the writings handed down to us, and broadly and sympathetically so. We are not here concerned with textual criticism; and though garnering treasures from the workshops of students and specialists, it is here desirable to only show the tendency and broad results which go towards forming a religion or philosophy.

For these and other reasons which the reader will better understand as he advances, our attempt to here give references for conclusions and summaries, as well as words and passages, became too complicated and cumbrous, and likely to alarm and deter most of those whom we desired to attract to this most interesting of studies, especially when viewed broadly, briefly, and not too ponderously. Those who desire to go deeper into the subjects will find all pretty fully treated of in our ten *Short Studies* just published, and of which this is the eleventh.

Though opening with Egypt, it must not be assumed that Egyptians had a religion before all others, but rather that they surpassed others in handing it down on more durable materials, and in the dryest of climates. Here, therefore, are perhaps the oldest of sacred writings — a ritual and great biblical literature, actually engraved over 5000 years ago, but which was "then so old as to be unintelligible to royal scribes." In consequence, it was even then the rule to "give the interpretation with the text;" and some sound Egyptologists think parts of this sacred *Ritual* were composed about 5000 B.C., when Egypt must have been a civilized state, with wondrous monuments of art and architecture, denoting great advance in astronomy, mechanics, hydraulics and other sciences, as well as in literature, poetry and painting.

Many of the wise maxims, precepts and teachings which are found in the writings of Ptah Hotep or Ani of 5000 years ago, and even of the age of the first pyramids, say, 6000 years ago, "appeal to the authority of the ancients," says M. Renouf in his *Hib. Lecs.* Even in these far back times we see many of our present rites, symbolisms and doctrines; as of a divine mediator, a dying and risen God, a Trinity, a death unto sin, and a life eternal, a Heaven, a Paradise or Ades; a millennium and final judgment, the observance of a sabbath, eucharistic fetes, lents and sacrifices, circumcision, baptism, and other mysteries; so that it is not strange to hear modern writers speak of the Hebrew bible having borrowed ideas and even passages from the "Ritual" or "Bible of the Nile."

Other religions treat more or less fully of similar matters, the value of which each reader will best appraise when all are thus grouped together. The latest faith should naturally be the best and most advanced. But whatever form the god or ideal takes, it is evident that the pictures on the canvases are merely the highest conception of each people at a particular period of their civilization. Ignorance or culture, climate and circumstances seem to have determined their hopes and desires, loves and fears, and therefore their gods, heavens and hells, faiths and philosophies; and not until man had reached a strictly scientific stage did he begin to brush aside the speculative and unknowable, and then very slowly and fitfully, but naturally.

With the view of testing such theories, we began many years ago to carefully study and collect all available data, not only from books, but many capable adherents of the ancient and modern religions of Asia with whom we held sympathetik intercourse for a third of a century. To this has been added laborious research, through the dusty tomes of bygone ages, and the following is a selection summarizing the views of many great leaders, so far as these dared to make their opinions public. If we are as accurate as we have tried to be in this chronological epitome, the reader will have before him a most valuable record of the growth of nearly all pious and philosophic thought from the earliest known times, down to Christianity—too well known to the majority of our readers to be here entered upon.

The summary embraces the deepest thoughts of the best and wisest of the world on man's past, present and future, and with the general result, that religions like all else have slowly and steadily evolved; that they never lept into existence through any supernatural agencies, and that their prominent great ones—*quasi* " divine founders "—were but the apex of pyramids which had been slowly maturing centuries or ages before their births. They but guided the currents of their time, and the streams flowed on assuming devious courses, concrete and sensuous forms none could stay or anticipate.

We are at no loss for the varied symbolisms of the Ideals, for wherever men have dwelt, hill tops are crowned with spired or domed shrines, vales and plains with fanes, altars or temples, rude, simple or gorgeous according to the culture of their votaries, and always correctly expressive of their feelings and ideas. In and around all these, whether in gloomy cell or cloister, under shady grove or bright canopy, the devotees knelt, prayed and wept, danced and loved; pouring forth their joys and sorrows from light or burdened hearts; and grave and cultured philosophers alone stood apart, or paced with placid step the sacred or academic grove, "porch" or *stoa*, condemning or contemning the credulity of their fellows; whilst pensive spirits like Buddha and others walked or knelt by lone mountain sides, mourning over the folly and depravity of man, his miserable or lost estate, and the vanity and unsatisfactoriness of all things.

EGYPTIAN RELIGIOUS THOUGHT
4000 TO 2000 B.C.

I

I am that which is, which will be, and no one yet
Has lifted the veil that covers me.
In contemplative silence we adore Thee.
Oh Thou Almighty and Incomprehensible One.
We see Thee placid and benign in all Thy works,
And know Thee as gentle in heart unto all creatures,
Yet we fear Thee as inexorably just.

II

Male and female art Thou—Nature's creative energies.
The Word and Wisdom; the Unbegotten with the Begotten One.
The Universe is Thee, and Thou speakest in its image.
Thou dissolvest, renewest, but never annihilatest.
We call Thee variously, Truth, Light, and Life,
And as a talisman wear Thy loved names on our breasts.

III

It is Thy name, the Everlasting—"I am that I am,"
The *Nuk pu Nuk* which we inscribe upon our dead.
For from Thee, the only Absolute holy existing One,
"All were," and by Thee again can they alone "be."

IV

Our divine amulets proclaim Thee true of speech,
The shield and mirror of all that is pure and good.
To the ignorant and profane we speak not of Thee,
'Twere to cast pearls before blind persons.

V

Before Thy temples we place the enigmatical sphinx.
And within—Gods, with fingers on lips.
Thy servant, Toth, could not conceive of Thee,
And our father, Amon, knew Thee as "The hidden One."
Thy personality, O Osiris, is intermingled with Rā,
And we call Thee God; for Thou art the One, and only One,
The sole Being who liveth for ever in truth and light.

VI

Thou alone hast not been made, but from Thee
Have all proceeded and to Thy bosom all return.
Thou art everywhere and always, in time and space,
Of one substance; the self-existent and unapproachable,
Yet manifest to us in divers forms and activities.
The Infinite, Ancient of days and universal Father,
Whose high behests we can neither resist nor delay.

VII

In all the divers forms with which men worship Thee,
The wise know Thee to be One God without a second;
The Eternal whom no Father created nor Mother bore:
The unbegotten God, goddess and creator of all existences.

VIII

Thou art the giver of our breath, life and light,
The sovereign of truth and judge of the poor and oppressed.
Thou alone knowest the heart and its secret springs,
Our hidden trials and unknown sacrifices;
And thou oft wipest the tear from off our faces;
Comforting when none seeth, and listening
When no man heedeth or pitieth us.

IX

Only with some few of Thy attributes
Can our finite intelligence hold communion.
It is to Thee that we offer our sacrifices,
The first fruits of our bodies, our flocks and vineyards.
For with Thee do we hope to spend an eternity of bliss
When, purified through many changing forms,
We lose our humanity in Thy dread impersonality.

X

We praise Thee for revealing Thyself unto us
In the sacred writings of Thy holy Toth.
In teaching us how to serve Thee here
That we may dwell with Thee for ever hereafter.

XI

We have given water to him who was athirst,
And clothing to those who were naked;
Have applied our hearts unto peace;
Been the father of the fatherless and support of the widow,
And sustained all who were true in heart.

XII

Thy servant allowed no misery, but feeding children
With corn, also instructed them in pleasantness of speech.
No overseers were harsh or rude nor oppressed the poor;
For I watched over all, and redressed every wrong,
And thus was strife prevented and my name loved.
Justice went beyond mere inaction and silence,
For none might veil their face from the hungry,
And wretchedness was unknown to widow or orphan.

XIII

We made no distinction between the known and unknown,
Nor regarded the favour of man in our judgements.
We have circumvented the evil doers,
And, shunning their society, have befriended
All who were fraudulently treated.

XIV

Thou, Great God, art the Lord of Heaven and Earth,
Who madest all things which are.
O my God and Lord, who hast made and formed me,
Give me an ear to hear and an eye to see Thy glories.
Thou Architect of the Universe, without Father or Mother;
A Father of Fathers, Begotten by Thine own Becoming,
The Mother of Mothers, born through repetition of Thyself;
The uncreated Watcher traversing the endless ages of Eternity.
Who watchest whilst all creation rests,
But who resteth not himself lest his people die.
Whose commands the heavens of heavens and earth obey,
Ever travelling by the roads thou hast laid down for them.

XV

O Ancient of Heaven! the God of truth and of wisdom,
The oldest of existences, and support of all who seek Thee;
Whose shrine is the secret place, and whose thoughts are hidden
Even from the gods around Thy throne.
Thou judge of the poor and oppressed, Lord of mercy and love,
The one without a second, "Hail to Thee from every land!"
The heights of heaven, and the depths of the sea proclaim Thee,
And to search for Thee, is the beginning of wisdom.

XVI

Our eternal hope is in Thee, Thou great Redeemer,
In Thy love, Thy death, and resurrection to glory;
For in Thy blood we are healed, justified and sanctified;
And as Thou, great Osiris, lived here a life of goodness
And suffering, rose—the first born of the dead—to live
The eternal judge of all men, so with confidence we,
Thy faithful followers, see our release from
The dread shades of Dark Amenti,
Into that "Land of the Rivers of Life."
A land like to this, but without sorrows and troubles,
Where, beside the fruitful "Tree of Life,"
We shall inhabit "Thy Mansions of Glory."*

XVII

Whilst at this vernal fete, realizing and rejoicing
In the beauties of this Thy fair creation,
Yet we neglect not to cast our eyes upon the silent dead,
Though clothed in fine raiment, and bedecked with jewels,

---

* "Osiris died only to rise again." Prof. Sayce's *Ancient Empires*, p. 62. What follows refers to the Annual Eucharistic Fête.

We remember that we must be swathed as mummies;
For we must seek Thee beyond the dread river of death,
And exchange the sweet odors, the perfumed oils,
The soft music and joyous scenes of earth.
For the fetid putrescence and silence of the tombs
Ere we can see Thy face and rejoice in Thee for evermore.

XVIII

Whoso beareth himself proudly God will abase.
For all that we have is His free gift.
Our children and treasures came alike from Him,
Therefore praise and laud His holy name.

XIX

Till thou that field which has been appointed unto thee,
And offer up secret prayers with a contented spirit.
Consider Him in all thy ways and let thy to-morrow be as to-day;
Give thyself up unto Him and He will order thy affairs:
Though he dwelleth in the sky, his emblems are on earth,
And it behoveth us therefore to meet and humbly adore Him.

XX

The orb of day proclaims Thee, and in contemplating its
Glories and attributes we worship the Creator of Eternity:
The August Spirit, Begetter of the gods, the Unknowable;
The Ancient One: the Mighty God who made and loveth us.
Who is like unto Ra-Osiris—thou all-embracing and Eternal One?

XXI

Help us to reach unto the Land of the Ages, the Eternal
Home which Thou destined for Thy righteous children.
I will praise Thee at thy rising in the golden east,

And worship Thee, God of Life and Light, at Thy crimson setting.
Who but Thee lighteth our paths through Earth's mazes;
Who guideth to the Elysian fields but Thee, O Osiris?

N.B.—Readers of Egyptian literature will here recognize many parts of the Bible of the Nile or *Ritual of the Dead*, where the Osirian pleads before his Lord's judgment seat with prayer and praise, reciting all the good deeds and intentions of his life on earth, as in *Ritual* cxxv., &c. Also many passages in *Records of the Past*, and the works of Bunsen, Birch, Lenormant, Renouf, Maspero, Ronge's *Monts.*, *Hib. Lecs.*, Bonwick, &c., &c., too numerous to quote.

CHINESE SCRIPTURES PRIOR TO CONFUCIUS

Compiled mostly by or through CONFUCIUS about 500 B.C., from the teachings of the patriarchal times of KING FU-HSI of 3270 B.C., "the founder of temples, sacrifices and arts." Also from "the Records of the Royal Sages, YĀU and SHUN of 2360 B.C. This Epitome constitutes a veritable

TURANIAN BIBLE

which in its quaint, homely, and practical phrazeology and absence of all speculative theories and theologies regarding the past and future, stands out in sharp contrast to all the Scriptures of Shemitik and Arian peoples. Its history and ancient foundations are fully dealt with in our *Short Study* VI.

I

Give your confidence to the virtuous, discountenance the artful;
Let none come between you and men of worth.

II

Good is not only good in itself, but leads to good fortune;
To neglect doing good is wicked, and leads others badly.

III

Study well all you purpose and by the light of reason,
And go not against the right, though it make thee unpopular,
Nor yet needlessly oppose any to gratify thine own desires.

IV

Make use of the ability and experience of those around thee;
And cultivate also men of worth though foreign and distant,
As well as the wisdom of ancient peoples.

V

Seek not enjoyment in idleness, nor in any excesses;
There are virtues and vices common to mankind,
Yet every one seeks, till corrupted, to be virtuous.
Neither goodness, evil ways nor words, can be long hidden;
Let all be impressed with thy search for, and love of virtue.

VI

The restless mind is prone to error and its affinity to right is small:
Oppress not the helpless nor neglect the weak and poor,
And observe the laws and customs of thy country.

VII

If a ruler, then caution men with firm but gentle words,
Yet correct when necessary with all the majesty of law;
Tempering judgment with mercy and forbearance,
And when doubtful, pausing; for it is better that the
Wicked should escape, than that the innocent be injured.

VIII

Whilst punishment must not extend to heirs of criminals,
Rewards may be handed down to many generations.
Pardon readily all inadvertent faults, yet punish
Purposed crimes however small, but with judgment.
Do not act on unsubstantiated words, but prove all things.

IX

Virtue and humility will move heaven.   Pride brings loss.
Combine affability with dignity; mildness with firmness;
Straightforwardness with gentleness and discrimination;
Boldness with sincerity, and valor with righteousness.

X

There is no stable model of virtue nor perfect type of goodness
But the uniform consciousness regulating its purity.

XI

Put away selfish thoughts, and seek not thine own ease;
Speak not in excess of the truth, and ever in a spirit of harmony.
Live but to labor for the enduring good of the people
And be not ashamed of faults, nor go on till they become crimes.

XII

It is not the *knowing* that is difficult, but the *doing*.
In learning be humble, but always earnest;
With learning will come virtue, though unperceived.
It is man, not heaven, who shortens life and adds misery.

XIII

Fear not the high and distinguished, but see rather that thou
Dost not oppress the friendless, childless, and orphans.

XIV

If Heaven seems against thee in our divinations, be still,
For activity may prove misfortune, and then the foolish scoff.
It is difficult to rely on Heaven, yet be reverential,
Fearing not to seek knowledge by every known means,
And ever zealously consistent in thy quest after truth.

XV

Be jealously watchful over small acts and words,
Lest they affect thy character in great matters.

XVI

The end of punishment is to make an end of punishment,
Therefore those persevering in villainy and treachery—those warring
Against the good of society, must not be spared;
Yet cherish not anger against the obstinate,
Nor show any that thou dislikest them.

XVII

Advance the interests of the good, and the bad will be improved,
All are born good, and evil comes from external circumstances.
Thou canst not find the same qualities in all,
Families which have long enjoyed high office and riches
Usually become wayward and dissolute.

XVIII

Widely diffuse knowledge and set a good example,
So that the ignorant and poor be made aware of their duties,
Their hardships are great and untranquilizing.

XIX

Knowledge and study will in the end purify thee,
Yet "is there no wise man, who is not also stupid."
A flaw in white jade may be ground away and forgotten,
But not so a flaw in thy speech. For it, naught avails.
Words are indeed thine own, but cannot be flung about;
Each will find its answer, as every deed will its reward.

XX

Say not this place is private, none can see me, but
Be free from shame in thine own chamber, as in public.

XXI

Look not for horns in the young ram, but know that
All effects are but conditions of their causes.

JAINISM OR YATI-ISM

SAID TO HAVE ARISEN 4000 TO 3000 B.C.

The present religions of Jainas, Jīns, Yins, Yanīs, Yatīs, or HERMITS, developed from pietists of prehistoric times, who retired to lone places, and sought to please and propitiate the powers of earth and skies by living hard ascetical lives, as seen in *Short Studies*, I. and II. *Yati-ism* was and is the first and last doctrine of Brāhmans, Tāotists, Buddhists, and all later sects of anchorites and monks, and was evidently the pious base on which arose the varied systems of Religions, with their divers rites, symbolisms and worships.

I

Separate thyself from the world, its ways, and vices,
Its distracting ambitions, lusts and vanities.
Associate only with the pious; with Srāmans,
Saints, and holy men devoid of worldly mindedness—
Those who dwell in lone places with contented minds;
Who seek no reward or praise from men, but an eternal
Restful *Nirvāna*;* freed from endless transmigrations,
And from the hells in which the wicked must be purified.

II

Only the lotus can grow in water and not be wetted by it.
Thou canst not live in, and not be of the world;
But strive to avoid its attachments, the cares of property
And of domestic life, and be chaste in heart as in conduct.
Circumstances and surroundings weigh down the strongest;
Seek out for thyself a path which will enable thee
To control the carnal man; induce a spiritual mind,
Meditation, ascetic tastes, and the pursuit of wisdom.

III

Eat sparingly and only the simplest foods of the poor,
Such as they may dole out with willing hearts.
Receive all without solicitation or remark,
Nay, with the indifference of a contented mind.
Seek not even medicines for thine ailments, and
Accept such resting-places as nature may provide,
Going forth, caring naught for house or home.
Sufficient to the Srāman is nature's earthen couch,
A garment of rags or none at all.

* This was an early Jaina term and idea; see our *Short Studies.* Dr Dahlmann calls it "pre-Buddhistic." *As. Qtly.*, April '97.

IV

Care not for what the worldly call cleanliness;
Remove no vermin from thy body or apparel,
But mercifully cherish all that has life.
Fan gently from thy path insect and worm,
For to destroy animal, yea plant life, is heinous sin.
On this account drink not cold water from spring or brook,
Nor light midst insect life, a fire even to cook thy food,
Nor breathe save through a cloth, lest aerial life be taken.

V

No true Jina joins in wars, or acts offensively to any:
He receives meekly rebukes, blows and persecution,
Answering not revilers or false accusations;
Nay, he accepts these as probably more or less true,
And inwardly strives to see his faults, and by more
Severe penances to curb his passions and desires.

VI

Only austere penance annihilates evil *karman*,
But let it be penance which none knoweth of:
That which is endured for fame has no merit,
But that is meritorious which is secret,
And is most repellent to thy nature.

VII

"No one becomes a *Srāman* merely by tonsure,
Nor a *Brāhman* by holy words and prayers,
Nor a *Muni*[1] by living in lone woods or caves."
Thou must show thy holiness by thy life, by doing justly,
Loving righteousness, by fulness of knowledge and equanimity.

---

[1] *Muni* and *Brāhman* were synonymous in these early Jaina days of Pârsva and Mahā-Vira, *S.B.E.*, xlv. 252. For meekness, see *Short Studies*, p. 27.

VIII

Leanness and nakedness is oft conjoined with deceit
And an irreligious heart. If thou wouldst be a
Brahman, prove it by delighting in goodness ;
For good conduct is better than words, rites or creeds.

IX

Study our "sacred and revealed texts," and the lives of Bodhas,
And strive diligently to walk in their footsteps ;
For life is a dark forest or trackless wilderness,
Where we must beware of false or blind guides,
Each leading according to his own desires.

X

Defilement cometh mainly from the heart and thoughts :
The chief sin is that which is knowingly committed :
That which is born of greed, pride, deceit and wrath.
Pleasures come not to those pursuing after them,
And miseries are usually the result of ignorance ;
Whilst carelessness causes much evil *karman*.

XI

Though renouncing the world, be not ignorant of it.
Know the truth and be heedful to live up to it.
Do all things carefully and in due order :
Have a time for eating, fasting, dressing and sleep :
For travelling, teaching, prayer and meditation :
For religious rites and thy Sabbaths or *Pásahas*.

XII

Strive after " Reciprocity "—doing as ye would be done by ;
For with what measure ye mete unto others,
Be it to man, beast or insect, nay, to plant life,
It will be measured to you in good or evil *karman*.

XIII

Attain unto purity of life, till evil be a burden to thee;
And seek strength by confessing thy faults to the wise
And by more strenuous efforts after holiness.
If vigilant, thou may attain to Sainthood, nay Nirvāna,
And by severe asceticism, meditation, and mental power,
Man may perchance reach the confines of Godhood.

XIV

But *Mŏksha*—" Absorption " or supreme blessedness—
Each can attain only by his own efforts,
Through knowledge, many experiences and penances.
Strive then to master thy *Karman* and heredity,
And gain Nirvāna, a state of rest and bliss,
Wherein is freedom from self, pain and mutation.

XV

Harbor no ill-will against any living creature,
And sternly avoid " the FIVE SINS " or *Ā-dharmas*,
Killing, lying, stealing, adultery and worldly-mindedness.

XVI

Thou must also fulfil " THE FIVE GREAT DUTIES."
I.—" Show mercy to all that has life.
II.—Give alms and aid freely to the needy.
III.—Venerate the Sages and their emblems.
IV.—Penitently confess all sins and faults.
V.—Observe all religious rites, texts and customs,"
And especially in prayerful humility the Lenten Services;
When the Sun of Righteousness having given to thee of his fruits,
Rests from labor on his autumnal couch.

XVII

It is not given to many to understand Life's mysteries ;
Yet confessing to the Unknown, perchance Unknowable,
The wise man seeks to comprehend the Known.
Granting that all beyond our experience is to us unknown,
He is here humbly silent like the Á-jnanakas,*
Fearing that to accept theories of the transcendental
Is but to speculate, beguile himself and the ignorant.

XVIII

Of this nature is the doctrine of spirits or souls.
None have seen these nor can prove if they exist.
We see only that words and actions are eternal,
Affecting all around us, and generations yet to come ;
That MATTER is supreme, unbegotten, and eternal ;
Producing Life, Mind, Intellect and Thought ;
Yea, a world infinite in forms and potentialities—
Offspring of its own latent and unknown energies.

XIX

Thus is the Universe or Matter, without beginning or end,
Constant only in its changes, physical and intellectual ;
Unformed and unsustained by any known creator or ruler,
Nor subject to the intervention of any power outside itself.

XX

Yet are there elements which develope almost to deities,
And which we have no faculties to comprehend either
The origin, essence or unconditioned state thereof.

* *Agnostics*—from *Jāna*, to know, showing that Prof. Huxley's apt term was used some millenniums ago.

XXI

Many call "the Five Gross Elements"—Earth,
Water, Fire, Wind and Air—original and everlasting;
Others name them "Earth, Water, Fire, Wind and *Atman*"—
The Self, Soul, Breath, Spirit or "Life Principle"—
(The *Jiva, Ruh, Napash, Psyché,* or *Pneuma* of many
Peoples), but still and originally, only "the Life-Breath;"
Born of the elements and inseparable from matter,
A function thereof, called its "Intelligent Principle."

XXII

We say: "The Five Elements were not created or made
Directly or indirectly. They were without beginning or
End, and the primary cause of all that is:"
We speak according to our knowledge and capacities,
And blame not those who worship spirits.

This has been carefully and principally gleaned from the Jaina Scriptures as given in the *S. B. of E.* series, the valuable writings from original sources of the indefatigable missionary, Dr Stevenson, and various Asiatic Journals, and our own intercourse with Jaina priests and pilgrims during a four years' residence in Western India. The scriptural sources belong to the 4th century B.C., when they appear as the teachings of *Mahā-Vira*, the 24th Jaina Bodha of 550 B.C., and of *Pārsva*, the 23rd of the 9th century B.C., and even then founded on the discourses and traditions of the 1st Bodha, Rishabha—heretofore thought to belong to the times of the Babylonian Akkads of 2500 to 3200 B.C. But if 200 years be reasonably allowed to each Bodha or Avatār, then Rishabha lived about 5000 B.C., a millennium after the Sumirs of Nipur built the temple to their god M'ul-lil or Al-lil, which scholars now agree with Prof. Hilprecht the explorer, "was somewhere between 6000 and 7000 B.C., possibly even earlier." (Prof. Sayce, *Contp. Rev.*, Jan. 1897.) Of course there were pious hermits, Yatis or Jinas long before gods were thought of and temples reared; see details in our *Short Studies*.

THE ZOROASTRIAN OR MAZDEAN SCRIPTURES
OF 1700 TO 500 B.C.

The following are gleanings from the pious and ethical teachings of the Āvastā-Zand Bible and other Authoritative Mazdāhan Scriptures.

I

Give to Thy Prophet and people, O Ahura, goodness and happiness,
And preserve us against all assaults of evil.

II

Sing the praises with me, of The One—The Living God
Who speaketh with us in the flames of the altar.
He is light, and its source, and shines on all alike,
The One Great Ruler from everlasting to everlasting.

III

Pray to Him without ceasing, and He will keep thee,
For He loveth the devout, and the "living wise ones."
Let all His commandments be dear to thee,
And seek after no God but Ahura the Mazdāo.
Hell is the portion of the unbeliever and wicked.

IV

Ahura alone can confound the evil doer
And give peace and joy to true believers.
He requireth good deeds, and piety doubles their value.
He giveth to the needy, as a friend to his friend.
Art thou helpless and in sorrow? Trust in Him
And aspire to live with Him for ever hereafter.

V

He is the Father of truth, the God of all goodness
Who resenteth all evil thoughts, words or deeds;
With Him dwell wisdom and piety, attended by truth;
And no evil one can abide in His presence.

VI

He is the fire of the mind by which all things are created.
Bow to His holy symbol, the *Āthar-Gāh* or Altar Fire;
And revere also the orbs of Heaven, for He shines in all.
He created them as well as Heavens, Earth and Waters.

VII

His holy Fire, and "Word" lived, ere our life was,
And moved before there was any day on the waters.
Then came "The Beginning" with Good and Evil, twin spirits.
Choose thou between these: thou canst not serve both—
Ahura Mazdā, the holy, and the evil Daēvas;
The Spirit of holiness, and the Originator of impurities.

VIII

Ahura requires thee to help forward the life of the future
By wise thoughts, words and deeds. As the tree is known
By its fruits, so is the good man by deeds and friends:
Associate with the righteous, and shun the paths of sinners;
Let no hypocrisy or untruth find in thee a friend.

IX

Search for wisdom as more valuable than all riches;
She alone is a shelter from lies and a fount of joy,
And the prudent make their home with her.
She confoundeth the wicked, giveth peace, and loveth righteousness.
Can clothe the individual with piety and all virtues,
And the state, with public and social happiness.

X

Seek after holiness of spirit and purity of mind and body,
Exhibiting these by conduct as well as by words.
Thou wilt find thy reward in thy heart, and mayhap in the love
Of some who honor the righteous; but hereafter thou
Wilt dwell with "the Spirits of the Perfected Just Ones,"
And with Ahura, "The Infinite Spirit" of the universe.

XI

In prayer we rejoice; in spirit we seek Thee, O God,
And pray that Thy kingdom may come quickly.
Let every sin which men have committed because of us,
And every sin we have committed because of men,
Be pardoned and forgotten by Thy mercy and grace.

XII

Remember Thy promises, that, in Thine own time,
Thou wouldest send thy Son, Holy SAÔSH-YANT,
The Unborn and Eternal One, the Judge and Lawgiver,
Who is to guide and lead us into all truth.
Then will this earth quake, and the dead arise;
Hell be destroyed, and the age of happiness be inaugurated.
The reign of *Angra Mainyu* and darkness will cease
And light and goodness triumph forever.

XIII

Ever and again will our lips repeat and hearts rejoice
In the *Ashem Vohu* or "Praise of Righteousness";
And reiterate the holy HURMAT, HUKHT, and HURVARST—
GOOD THOUGHTS, GOOD WORDS, and GOOD DEEDS.
By these only can true Religion and the good man be known,
Not by prayers, worship, rites, and sacrifices.

XIV

Whoso looketh for salvation here and hereafter,
Must wage continual warfare with evil;
Have a pure mind, and a body free from defilement,
And feed the Spirit on words of truth and holiness.

XV

He must seek aid in ordinances, and make even the simple
Daily offices of life remind him of duties and works of piety.
Thus in changing the *Kusti* five times a day he will
Be reminded of the five prayers, duties and acts of grace.
When seeing fire, sun and sea, he should think of the Creator,
Yet must he not look on these, or aught else in earth
Or skies, when addressing AHURA the MAZDA.

XVI

Whoso loveth Ahura careth kindly for all his creation,
Treating justly and tenderly man and beast; nay all
Sentient creatures, nor by hasty word or deed paineth he any.

XVII

Commit to memory and ponder ever on Heaven's "Divine Law,"
And pray to Ahura for an understanding heart.
He spoke unto Zarathustra the words of Eternal Life;
And from Him and no priest came our *Dîn* or "Revelation."
He is rich in love; heavenly amongst the heavenly;
And has pardoned the sins of some even in hell,
How much more of those who excel in good works?

XVIII

Be sincere ; for Ahura abhorreth hypocrites ;—
Those who make long prayers but harbor evil thoughts ;
Who practise evil ways and are the associates of sinners.

XIX

Ahura loveth to reward the righteous
And to give peace to him who renounces sin :
His motto is that " Perfect Excellence is Righteousness."
The *Ahura Vairya* telleth of " His ever abiding Presence,"
The *Yatha Vairyo*, of " His Law of Holiness " ; and He,
The " Eternal Guide," is the Alpha and Omega of our Faith.

ORPHEANS

OF 14TH TO 6TH CENTURY B.C.

Next in chronological order may be placed some of the religious and kosmikal ideas which have come down to us embodied in ancient hymns and poems, commonly recognized in classic times as those of Orpheans, and variously placed at from 1400 to 500 B.C. They were believed to have been composed and sung by more or less mythical sages like Orpheus, Olen Linus, Musæus, or " the Orphik Brethren " generally ; and they were accepted as good and true religious teachings by writers of the Homeric and Hesiod type, and by many schools of thought down to Plato and Neo-Platonists. Some attributed them to Puthagoras and his Jaino-Buddhistik schools, but they lack the calm, dry, realistic and moral ring of the early Buddhists. Their gods, spirits, and spiritual matters point rather to early sects of Jaina Bodhists.

I

There is but one Intellect, the Supreme, " the Good,"
Who comprehends the world in his infinite nature,
He manifests himself through three great Demiurgic principles,
The Jovial, Dionusiakal, and Adoniakal,
Which some call Mundane, Super-Mundane, and Generative,
Others, " Gods " and forces necessary to Nature's purposes.

II

The male and female is in all things; even the Heavens and the Earth.
For does not Earth receive the celestial defluxions,
And so produce all its varied life,
Each after its kind, animal and vegetable?

III

" Even the universe great Jove contains,*
The ether bright and heaven's exalted plains,
Th' extended restless sea, and earth renown'd,
Ocean immense and Tartarus profound;
Fountains and rivers, and the boundless main,
With all that Nature's ample realms contain,
And gods and goddesses of each degree;
All that is past, and all that ere shall be,
Occultly and in fair connection lies
In Jove's wide womb, the ruler of the skies.

. . . . .

ONE is the Pow'r Divine, in all things known,
And one the ruler, absolute, alone.

. . . . .

* Taylor's *Orphik Hymns*—London, 1787, are here to the point.

IV

See how his beauteous head and aspect bright
Illumine heaven, and scatter boundless light,
Round which his pendant golden tresses shine,
Form'd from the starry heavens, with light divine.
On either side two radiant horns behold,
Shap'd like a bull's, and bright with glittering gold." *

V

The Sun ruleth over phenomena and Apollo over noumena,
But "the Good One" ranges over all intelligence.

VI

There are worlds beyond ours where, as in *Mené*,
There exist mountains, cities, and houses of lunarites.
To us, Sol is "the Bull-horned one," and Selenê, "Mother of Ages;"
"Female and male, who with borrowed rays doth shine,
Now full-orbed, now tending to decline."

VII

Go pray to the deities of the ethereal orbs,
Offering sweet oblations, incense, and manna.
Saying unto the Sun, "as the Lord God of Hosts"—
"Hear, golden Titan, whose eternal eye,
With broad survey, illumines all the sky,
Self-born, unwearied in diffusing light,
And to all eyes the mirror of delight.

. . . . .

With thy right hand the source of morning light,
And with thy left the 'Father of the Night.'

. . . . .

* According to Dr Cudworth, "we have here the Grand Arkanum of Orphik Theology, as in *Proclus in Timæus.*"

VIII

Foe to the wicked, but the good man's guide,
O'er all his steps propitious you preside.
With various sounding golden lyre 'tis thine
To fill the world with harmony divine.
Father of ages, guide of prosperous deeds,
The world's commander borne by lucid steeds;
Immortal Jove, all-searching God of light,
Bearer of fruit, Almighty Lord of years,
Agile and warm, whom every power reveres;
Great eye of nature and the starry skies,
Doomed with immortal flames to set and rise;
Dispensing Justice, lover of the stream.
The world's great despot, and o'er all supreme.

. . . . .

Propitious on these mystik labours shine,
And bless thy suppliants with a life divine."

IX

Who is man that he should separate nature from God,
Or "Providence" from nature—"The Eternal Mother"?
Worship thou her as the demiurgic cause of the
Whole sensible world; humbly fumigating
Her altars with thy choicest aromatics,
And chanting to her thus in divine verse.

X

"Nature—All-parent, ancient and divine,
O much mechanic mother, art is thine.
Immortal, First-born, ever still the same
Nocturnal, starry, shining, glorious dame.

. . . . .

Finite and infinite, alike you shine
To all things common, and in all things known,
Yet incommunicable and alone.

XI

Without a father of thy wondrous frame,
Thyself the father, whence thine essence came,
All flourishing, connecting, mingling soul
Leader and ruler of this mighty whole.

. . . . .

Ethereal, earthly, for the pious glad,
Sweet to the good, but bitter to the bad.
Father of all, great nurse and mother kind,
Abundant, blessed, all spermatik mind;
Mature, impetuous, from whose fertile seeds
And plastic hand, this changing scene proceeds.

. . . . .

Immortal Providence, the world is thine,
And thou art all things, Architect divine."

N.B.—Much of the ethics and pious thoughts of these singers occur in the teachings of other and later schools: see especially under Puthagoras, Herakleitos, etc.; but the above shows a highly developed worship of nature, elemental and solar.

HINDUISM—VEDAS AND VEDĀNTISM
1400 B.C.—400 A.C.

We keep very close to the Scripture Texts, so this may be truly called in those pre-Purānik times—

THE BIBLE OF HINDUS

I

Many and divers are the names men give Thee,
But the wise know Thee as only one Being
The *Ekam eva ad vitiyam*, or "one without a second";
Nature, Providence, The Supreme and everlasting essence.
"He who is" and moves—"the Thinker of Eternal thoughts,"
Which only the wisest can apprehend.
Our eye cannot behold thee, or mind picture thee,
Speech is indeed dumb, or wasted in hollow words
Which striveth to pourtray thee.

II

We worship thee in the ethereal sky, sun, nature and fire,
For thou wert the golden child in the beginning of Time;
The first-born and sole spirit of all things;
The breath of life, source and strength of gods and men,
That which *was*, before heavens and earth *were*.—

III

Before aught, yea naught existed, "Thou wert
The only One, breathing breathless by *Itself*
And other than *Itself*, has nothing ever been."
Only "The All in All" know'st whence creation came
Or perchance Thou knew not and wert mute.

IV

Our thoughts cannot depict Thee, and in words we vainly say
"Thou art a first cause yet without a cause";
The soul of the universe and Father of NATURE—
The Self-produced and producing, who operates through all.

V

Thou too art in all that exists in space and time;
The light of lights without eye or ear;
Who yet seest and hearest all—Thyself invisible,
Impersonal, but breathing on all, though breathless,
And speaking clearly to all, though voiceless.
We have no faculties to comprehend Thy Infinity,
Enough, that "Thou arose, wished, and all things were."

VI

"Thy loving kindness is light, and Thy shadow death,"
And the good man lives reposefully on Thy spirit.
Of fathers thou art the most fatherly, our loving friend and guide,
Of mothers, the pitiful heart which seeketh after the lost ones.
Thou sendest thy messenger—the Lord of Light, unto us,
And urgest all to worship thee with a cheerful heart.
Agni is thy spirit, wafting our supplications on high,
And calling upon us to be "pure in heart and sin not.

VII

O Giver of life and immortality, show thyself unto us
Throughout all the troubles and trials of our lives.
As we pass through the watery wastes of earth and skies,
Let thy spirit in a still small voice speak within us;
So that, when freed from sin and flesh on the consuming pyre,
We may arise pure spirits to dwell for ever with thee
In those blessed and bright abodes of the righteous,
Where rest the spirits of the just made perfect in thy spirit.

VIII

We know thou abhorest the ways of unjust men,
Neither giving to them felicity here nor hereafter.
But the contented spirit who resisteth evil,
Curbing all sensual appetites, wrath and covetousness;
Who injureth not his fellows nor pursueth after gain,
Who delighteth in a knowledge of Thee and his Vedas,
Who hath controlled his affections and calmed his mind—
That man hath broken the fetters which bound him to life,
Hath inherited Brahmă; and dwelling in him
Is dead unto the flesh and has all but attained immortality.

IX

We long to dwell in the secret place of the Most High,
Where life is free and the heavens radiant with His light,
Where the imperishable One shineth as the sun:
There indeed is true happiness, and "the desire of our desires
Is gratified" in thy abiding presence, O Lord Prajăpati.—

X

Let us not, O Varuna, enter the house of clay:
Have mercy, O Almighty, have mercy.
We are weak and have sinned, Thou ever Strong One:
Have mercy, O Lord, have mercy.
Through thoughtlessness have we broken Thy laws:
Have pity, O Brahma, have pity.
Give unto us the spirit of love and prayer:
Have mercy, O Lord, have mercy.
Our souls are overwhelmed by great waters:
Have mercy, Almighty One, have mercy.
Though surrounded by waters, we are athirst:
Have pity, O Lord, have pity.

XI

He who considereth Thy perfections in devout abstraction,
Who resteth not on his own understanding, works or virtues,
Who liveth uninfluenced by the world and illusions of time,
He cannot sin but dwelleth with Thee for ever.

XII

Naught can be done without or apart from Thee;
Right and Truth, Light and Darkness are Thy handmaids,
And only as we serve Thee, can we obtain their aid.
Thou art Dyaūs surrounded by the Devas or "Light ones";
An Ouranos whose ethereal covering shelters us.

XIII

We see Thee in our earliest Trinity or Trimūrti.
In Aryman, Varūna and Brahmā, as well as in Vishnu
And Mitra or Sūrya, "The glowing and resplendent one."
In these "three persons, the one god is shown,
  Each first in place, each last, not one alone.
  Of Siva, Vishnu, Brahmā, each may be
  First, second, third, among the blessed three."

XIV

Loving all we hymn the praises of all,
But especially of "the swift courser"—"the Hunter"
Who pursueth ever his kindly, bounteous race;
Quickening our flocks and herds;
Fortifying our young men and maidens,
And enriching our lands with corn and oil.

XV

To Thee, thou mighty Triune, Lord of all
We offer the first-fruits of all things;
All are Thine, and we are Thy children;
And bending our bodies in humblest adoration,
We intone in sweetest harmony our hymns of praise.

XVI

O, Thou great Triune, Ruler of Time and Destiny,
Thou who wert praised, ere even Vedas were,
In hymns our old men called " Ancient Songs."
Thou who knowest our most secret thoughts
And numberest every wink of men's eyes,
Whose countless messengers, angels and archangels
(Cherubim and seraphim) pervade all space ;
In whose hands we are but feeble worms,
Forgive us all our sins and negligences,
And grant unto us peace, joy, and plenty.

XVII

In thy sight the very " hosts of heaven " are unclean,
And wait upon Thee with songs and sacrifices, yea
" The Lord of creation offered Himself in sacrifice for the gods,"
Believing that without blood there could be no remission of sin.

XVIII

So Parūsha—the primeval male was sacrificed to Thee
For Thy glorious and eternal creation of all things.
Thus in our childhood we offered the innocent for the guilty,
Yea, the fruit of our bodies for the sin of our souls :
But now we offer only oblations on thy altars,
The choicest products of our fields and vineyards,
Convinced that thou abhorest the blood of victims,
And that sacrificial posts but pollute thy sanctuaries.

XIX

We rejoice that our spirits thus hold communion with Thine,
And that, like Thine, our souls too are immaterial—
Unborn and Eternal—inferior only to thine immortal
Holy Spirit, in wisdom, reason, and knowledge.

XX

As with us, in Thy mind, too, "was formed desire—"
That primeval productive germ which, the wise say
Is the subtle bond connecting entity with nullity;
For "out of nothing, nothing comes," and hence
Matter too, like spirit, was with Thyself eternal;
Yet not so creature-life, for in Thy awful loneliness
Thou didst long for another, and forthwith falling in twain
Was consummated Thy glorious incarnation—
 "THE ARDHA NĀRI ĪSWARA!"

XXI

From this "*duo in uno*"—an active receptive double
Of one flesh, thou didst produce male and female like unto us,
Gods and goddesses and sons and daughters of men.
Thus didst Thou make known Thy glory and loving-kindness,
As well as that holiest institute of earthly bliss,
The happy union of two loving spirits.

XXII

Thou, "Lord of Worlds," art yet very near to each one of us,
Thou seest us when we walk or stand by the way,
And knowest our down-sittings and uprisings;
Yea, the thoughts of our hearts, as well as our words.

XXIII

The whisperings of bosom friends are all heard by Thee,
Nay, Thou countest the very twinklings of our eyes;
Nought is too small nor too great for Thy care,
Nor too distant for Thy loving supervision.
Could we flee beyond oceans and skies, Thou art there,
For they are Thy loins, O great Varūna;
Yet Thou dwellest in every pearly drop of water—
The universal life and light and soul of all,
The all-pervading essence in which the world is absorbed.

XXIV

When nought was, neither entity nor non-entity,
Thou "The I am" breathed, "yet without afflation." *
In darkness and chaos Thou wert "unseen light,"
Ever "Pure Wisdom," the Infinite Logos, the Unchangeable,
A spirit without matter, parts or passions,
Omnipotent, everlasting, and the incomprehensible.

XXV

Thou sittest aloof, neither interested nor moving;
Watchful only as the mirror is to receive shadows—
An ever cold and passive beholder of unalterable Law;
Calm and solitary in Thy unembodied unity.

XXVI

It was Thy Spirit, impressed Mâya or "Mirrored Illusion,"
That something, yet nothing; real only as the cause of all,
Yet unreal for existing not as a Being;
Untrue, for without essence, though existent as Thy power—
A part of Thy imperishable Soul, embodied in illusion,
And waiting but for a few days to return to Thee again.

XXVII

As the rains descend, form rivers, and run to the Ocean,
So Thy spirit descends as life and merges again in Thee.
Thou art moisture in the water; the light in the sun;
The sweet scent of the flower; and the harmony of the spheres.

---

* This divine term for deity, "the I am" or "He Is," occurs primarily among Egyptians. *Cf.* Max Müller's *India, what it Teaches*, p. 248.

N.B.—Hindus and European scholars will readily recognise the writings from which we have culled these SHORT TEXTS, especially after reading *Short Studies*, IV., on Vedas and Vedantism. It would have been impossible, as elsewhere explained, to have given all references; but to show how close we have kept to the actual texts, we may here give an authoritative translation from the *Atharva Veda*, reminding us of the Heb. Psalm cxxxix.: "Varuna, the Lord of these worlds, sees as if he were near.... If a man stands or walks or rides; if he goes to lie down or get up.... What two people sitting together whisper, Thou, O Varuna, knows it; thou art there as a third.... The two seas—the sky and ocean—are the loins of Varuna, yet is He contained in the smallest drop of water. He who flees far beyond the sky, even he would not be rid of Varuna the Lord.... He counteth even the twinklings of our eyes," etc. It is to avoid such wearying reading that these *Short Texts* are composed.

HOMER THE IONIAN

9TH TO 7TH CENTURIES B.C.

Great Zeus is the omnipotent and supreme,
His rod is the fiat of destiny.
Yet laws and circumstances even control Him
Who guides the decrees of fate.

All good as well as evil proceeds from Jove,
Justice and mercies, blessings and curses.—
Transient, mortal and finite to us here,
But eternal, immortal and infinite hereafter.

There is not much religious matter bearing on our purpose to be got out of Homer, beyond this doctrine of a God and a hereafter.

THALES OF MILETUS

FL. 600 B.C. (640-546)

All things must have had a beginning,
And primarily there must have been water and heat ;
For without these, naught can germinate.
So gods are said to move or develope on water,
Else would even their creative energy be vain.
It is meet to speak humbly of "The Great Unmade One,"
He who is necessarily the oldest of all existences.
He requireth us to execute justice, mercy and goodness,
Not to do unto our fellows what
We would blame them for doing unto us.

ANAXIMANDER

FL. 570 B.C. (610-532)

I

How can matter, a concrete, elemental substance,
Be the absolute or ultimate beginning of all things ?
It is at the most an existence *per aliud*,
And an eternal existence must exist *per se*.
The primary being must necessarily be a unity,
Though, being One, it may have the potentiality of All.

II

The ultimate origin of matter and all things is *the Arché*—
The Beginner, the *To Apeiron* or Infinite,
A divine and everlasting, absolute unity—mayhap
Spiritual and intelligent, and the substance by
Which all is formed, and into which all dissolves.

III

The *Apeiron* is neither fire, air nor water,
But a something common to both.
Out of chaos it organized all homogeneous particles—
Monads or atoms having affinities towards each other.
Thus did the earth and planets become spheres of concentric
Layers, ever increasing from encircling water and air,
Which produced first aquatic and then land organisms.

IV

All the spheres are populated like to our earth,
And the central solar fire heats and lights all.

LĀO-TSZE, THE FOUNDER OF TĀO-ISM
FL. 560 B.C. (604-515)

The following is a summary of the leading ethical teachings of this wise and highly devout sage, gleaned from his life-long discourses and authoritative TĀO-TEH-KING, and well authenticated writings of disciples, as set forth in *Short Studies*, V. There was fully explained the sage's term TĀO for his rather "incomprehensible" God; and we may therefore call the *Lāo-tsze-king* or

BIBLE OF TĀO-ISM
(THE SECOND TURANIAN SCRIPTURES)

I

Tāo is primordial reason, law and intelligence;
Tāo formed, controls and rules the world.
It is Î, for it cannot be seen;
It is HÎ, and thou canst not hear it;
It is WEI, therefore cannot be felt;
It is Three in One and an inscrutable mystery.

II

Tāo produced one, the one, two; and two, three;
And from Three proceeded all beings.
Many speak of Tāo who know it not,
Those who know it best, seldom speak of it.

III

"The reason which cannot be reasoned
Is not the divine and eternal reason;
The name which cannot be named
Is not the eternal name."

IV

The virtuous man is like water on a thirsty land,
Spreading blessings wherever he goeth;
Ever doing good and content therewith,
Seeking no reward, not even to please himself.

V

Strive with none, save to excel in human tenderness:
By this is the strength of the strong and wise man seen.
Compassion cometh from above, and the noblest masculine
Nature is that which also preserves much of the feminine:
By the conjunction of these the world is knit
Together in the holy bonds of sympathy and friendship.

VI

Show affection and tenderness to all living creatures,
Especially the helpless, widows and orphans.
Actively rescue those who are in peril,
Sympathize with the bereaved and afflicted,
And rejoice when the good man prospereth.

VII

Be moderate and frugal that thou may'st be liberal,
And in all circumstances, true, gentle and humble.
It is the greatest rivers which run softly and at lowest levels,
And on their banks, nations and peoples seek to
Dwell, amid peace and plenty—heaven-given bounties.

VIII

Be compassionate to errors, and brave against wrongs:
Return good for evil; truth for insincerity;
Gentleness for wrath. Seek the good of the evil doer and
Strive for reconciliation, but urge not thine own wrongs,
Else will there ever remain a grudge behind.

IX

Impute not wickedness to any, especially to the unfortunate;
Nay, think well of all, and reject not even the bad,
For they must be brought back to *Tāo*—the Divine Way.
They are the materials on which the good man works.

X

Wickedness is mostly due to circumstances and ignorance:
Remedy these and expose errors with kindly sympathy,
And the greatest wanderer may be won to Tāo.
But example is more valuable than precept,
And a pure act of self-denial or submission
Is worth thousands of free exercises of the will.

XI

Quiescence and a policy of inaction is often a high duty
In government as well as social turmoil.
By silence and doing nothing, we throw more responsibilities
Upon the disturbers—their leaders and the sufferers.

Though apparently passive, the gentle and soft can
Overcome the hard; so water—the softest of all things—
By continual minute dropping, weareth away rocks,
And by entering quietly into unseen or minute fissures,
Mollifies the hardest and finally overthrows mountains.
It thus reforms and renews the whole earth,
And brings into existence fresh growths and modifications.

XII

He who can perceive small things or mere influences
Is clear-sighted; but let him gently use his powers.
The attributes of Tāo seem to us often babe-like,
But a good government is one which is little seen or felt.
Laws but distract and impoverish the people, who should
Learn to guide and transform themselves.
The meddlesome is usually an intolerant government,
Making the governed restless and disobedient;
The consciously strong can afford to seem weak,
And thus rule without any appearance of force.

XIII

Learning and knowledge cause unrest alike to the State
And individual, for learners are never content till they know all,
And there is no greater calamity than discontent.
The learned do not usually know Tāo;
It is revealed to babes—the simple pious ones.
Child-like, and in thine own closet seek after Tāo;
It is only revealed to the restful, spiritual heart,
And whoso gaineth it, though he die, perisheth not.

XIV

Neither seek nor fear death, but thy appetites and passions;
The meshes of heaven's net are large, but none escape.

XV

He who lightly asserts, rarely keeps his word.
Weigh well all the difficulties thou mayst encounter,
Then shall no difficulties overcome thee.

XVI

Not to know our own ignorance is a fatal disease,
As also to fancy we know, when we know not;
To fear not, when and what we ought to fear,
It is to live in the fool's Paradise and to court evil.

XVII

Revere the *Tão-Teh* and believe in all its teachings,
Walking in all the ways it commands.
In this regard not man nor any obstacles,
Nor let thy zeal flag as thy days are prolonged.
Study it when thou risest from thy bed,
And when thou sittest down, ponder well its truths,
Treasuring up all its maxims in thy heart.
Be not ashamed to speak of it even on the house top;
So shall happiness possess thy heart and household,
And thy days and end be bright and peaceful.

XVIII

Those neglecting Tão, vainly seek salvation in learning,
Even in works of benevolence and righteousness.
Their pursuits are vanity, falsely called wisdom,
Which the world would be better and happier without.
They pursue artful contrivances for luxury and gain,
Which the Tãoist eschews. It is better indeed that
The people remain in their pristine ignorance and innocence.

XIX

Busy not thyself merely with the things of time;
Even the goodness of doing good is not real goodness.
Rule wisely thy spirit and judge not thy neighbors;
Suffice for thee to know well thine own self;
To be chaste, and not the contentious chastener of others.
Let not purity in words and deeds satisfy thee,
But be pure in mind and intentions:
Then only attempt to guide or influence others.

XX

What men or the world reverence, treat reverently.
Good words gain popularity, and good deeds, friends.
The wise accept peaceably many grievances,
And he who is contented has conquered himself.

XXI

Murmur not at the decrees of heaven,
Nor neglect any of the duties of thy station.
Honor thy parents and all in authority over thee,
And though thy pathway is beset by evil spirits
Within thine own bosom and beyond thee,
Yet walk fearlessly, remembering that good spirits
Are also overseeing and watchfully protecting thee.

We may conclude with Lord Tennyson's words in his short poem of 1885 upon this good sage's teachings:—

"Let be thy wail and help thy fellow-men,
And make thy gold thy vassal, not thy king,
And fling free alms into the beggar's bowl,
And send the day into the darken'd heart;

Nor list for guerdon in the voice of men,
A dying echo from a falling wall;
Nor care—for Hunger hath the Evil eye—
To vex the noon with fiery gems, or fold
Thy presence in the silk of sumptuous looms;
Nor roll thy viands on a luscious tongue,
Nor drown thyself with flies in honied wine;
Nor thou be rageful, like a handled bee,
And lose thy life by usage of thy sting;
Nor harm an adder thro' the lust for harm,
Nor make a snail's horn shrink for wantonness;
And more—think well! Do-well will follow thought,
And in the fatal sequence of this world
An evil thought may soil thy children's blood;
But curb the beast would cast thee in the mire,
And leave the hot swamp of voluptuousness
A cloud between the Nameless and thyself,
And lay thine uphill shoulder to the wheel,
And climb the Mount of Blessing, whence, if thou
Look higher, then—perchance—thou mayest—beyond
A hundred ever-rising mountain lines,
And past the range of Night and Shadow—see
The high-heaven dawn of more than mortal day
Strike on the Mount of Vision!
     So, farewell."

PYTHAGORAS, THE WESTERN PUTHU-GURU.

"The Samian Sage." Fl. 545 b.c.

I

Strive to be as virtuous, good and perfect as possible,
Yet remember humbly that thou art no better than others.
Heaven has gifted thee with *Nous* and *Phrenes*—Reason and Mind;
Yet dost thou differ only in degree from other animals.
They too have *Nous* with *Thumos*, mind, soul and courage,
And senses, often earlier and superior to their own;
But they lack thy voice and higher potentialities;
Improve then thy advantages, for the uncultured man
Is but little removed from the brute creation.

II

All creatures must undergo transmigration;
The vicious in Tartarus, till purified for heaven.
Strive after knowledge by which come virtues,
And train thyself by study in contemplative silence
Slowly and through many years; opening not thy mouth
Till thou canst instruct and benefit mankind.

III

Chasten the body if thou wouldst advance the soul;
Abstaining from much or strong foods and wines,
And from all exciting and untranquilizing scenes.
Thou need'st not flesh, and ought not to injure life,
Especially cattle, which till thy fields and feed the young.

IV

Yet maintain thy body in full vigor by air and exercise;
The gymnasium as well as study is necessary to man,
For a healthy mind is rarely found in a weakly body;
Both equally require sustenance and avoidance of
All excesses—carnal, physical and mental.

V

So live till a quiet, good and useful life becomes natural to thee,
And let it be helpful to the busy toilers around.
Seek not to be their ruler, but *philosophos* and guide,
For this is the highest rôle of the wise and good.

VI

Sympathize with all and actively aid the oppressed;
Thou wilt have thy reward in inward peace and joy.
True happiness can come unto us in no other way;
It is the offspring of virtue, sympathy and brotherly kindness.

VII

Seek self-improvement by keen nightly introspection,
Weighing well the day's thoughts, words and actions.
Ask thyself daily: " What have I learned, seen and heard,
What know I more, that's worth the knowing,
What have I done, that's worth the doing,
What have I sought, that I should shun,
What duty have I left undone,
Or into what new follies run." *
These self enquiries never cease
To lead to virtue and to peace.

* Mr J. Adams' translation of "*The Golden Lines.*"

VIII

We are mere ephemeræ, subject to metempsychoses,
Yet are our words and deeds more or less eternal
And will live down the ages for good or evil.
Weigh these therefore well, and see they be true and just,
And above all things conscientious and faithful.

IX

Be diligent in pursuit of all knowledge, especially
The sciences of the earth and heavens; mathematics and
Numbers will enable thee to grasp astronomy—the
Harmony of the universe, and the music of the spheres—
That eternal rhythmic cadence unknown to the ignorant;
But which the scientific perceive in the eternal course
Of suns and planets sweeping through their orbits.

X

Religion tells of the *Apeiron* or Infinite—"the Archê,"
The Divine Beginner; the Power behind phenomena;
The Absolute *Nous* or Intelligence; the Eternal Soul
Of the Kosmos; of Law and Order; without form or passions.
This is inaccessible to our senses, yet conceivable to the intellect,
As filling the etherial space of a heavenly Olumpos.

XI

From this Infinite, radiates productive fires and all light,
Sustaining our *Gé* and *Ouranos*, Space and Time.
Our very souls are parts of the infinite soul,
A something, neither rational nor irrational,
But which returns again to the universal soul,
When the body returns to its primordial dust.

XII

Seek not to please the *Arché* by rites and sacrifices,
But by a pure heart and by living up to thy highest ideal.
He sees and pervades all space, and all thou hast is from Him;
Yet mayest thou offer, on unstained altars, the fruits
And beauties of thy fields with a thankful heart;
For this calleth forth thine own and children's gratitude,
And worketh for good in its reflective attitude.

XIII

Our deity is a unity limited, like ourselves, by matter,
Which "He strives to conduct to the best of purposes,"
As thou too, must, till thy soul is absorbed in the universal.

XIV

In matter we can see monads—all but invisible cells
Without magnitude or extension, yet pervading all space,
And moving in marvellous combinations according to
Invariable modes and laws which we can trace
And calculate, but neither fathom nor comprehend.
Fire, light and moisture are clearly the motors or agents
Hence deified by the ignorant as the creators of worlds;
For truly earths like ours may crowd all space, each more
Organized as they reach unto the perfected Olumpos.

THEOGONIS OF MEGARA

FL. 540 B.C. (580-490?)

Do no ill to any, consideration becomes the just:
When thy neighbor acknowledges his fault,
Restore him cheerfully to thy friendship.

Justice and righteousness embrace all virtues collectively:
Choose these though they lead thee to trouble and poverty;
Misery must eventually pursue the unjust man but not
Him who acts sincerely and helpfully towards his fellows.

GÖTAMĀ "THE BUDDHA," OR SĀKYA THE MUNI

FL. 517 B.C. (557-477)

This great founder of a religion, which has more adherents than any other, started as a pious ascetik of the then all-pervading Jaina Bodhism, that earliest phase of piety which consisted of withdrawal from the world to the life of a *Yati* or hermit, Jīna or Jaina. Gôtama only began to realize the higher Buddhism or "Wisdom" in his mature manhood. Like many religious men, he passed through divers emotional stages, awakening from "a worldly" life to a pious sense of sin, but also to a somewhat pessimistic belief in the vanity of all things. These were also stirring times not only in India, but everywhere—one of those cyclic periods depicted in the chart of *Rivers of Life*. The sixth century B.C. had at Buddha's birth opened with the Agnostic "*Six Darsanas*" or philosophies of the schools of the great metaphysician and Rishi *Kapila*, the neighbor and probable tutor of the rising Buddhist avatāra.

Rishi Kapila had then been long writing and teaching—inspired, it was believed, by Vishnu—in the revered groves on the banks of the sacred *Kohini* by the waters of which, in a lovely garden, Māyā had given birth to a greater than even the aged philosopher of Kapila-Vastu.

As Gôtama grew up, his thoughtful nature became greatly touched by life's miseries, and by the *atheistic* heresies of the philosophers. In vain did his anxious father, *Sud-dhadana*, try to overcome the fears and resolves of his *Sid-dhārta*, or the "one in whom all the aims or hopes" of his kingdom centred. Gôtama refrained from all independent action until he was of age, had married, and had a son; when, like many pious Brâhmans, he became a *Vāna-prastha*, or "Forest recluse." He then, about 540 B.C., forsook his father's Court, and retired to the forest of Rāja-griha in the kingdom of Behār, by paths still everywhere marked in the memories of half Asia. He settled at Bôdha Gayā, some 120 miles easterly from Banāras, and about 250 from his home.

Here he strove for several years to follow in the faith of his Fathers, and to suppress the ever disturbing truths which the *Vedānta* and *Nyāya* or logical schools, but especially the *Sānkhya* philosophy of Kapila, had brought home to him. Believing that the flesh was the destroying element of our higher nature, he would have perished in his ascetic life but for Hindus going about feeding such hermits.

So Buddha lived for about five or seven years, as did his western counterpart Pythagoras (another "Pūtha-gūrū"), Apollonius of Tyana, and others.

Under the sacred Bo-tree at Gayā, Gôtama studied and taught all comers, until "he obtained enlightenment," and became famous in his small circle as "The Buddha" or "Wise One"; and this is what we call his FIRST STAGE, the second being that of an active pious philosopher, ever going about doing good. Then it was that he thrust aside all egoistic thoughts, and leaving his forest retreat, started for the great world of Banāras, determined to do his best to regenerate mankind. Then, as now, there was endless speculation regarding immortality, the existence and nature of a soul, &c., but on these dark speculative matters Buddha ever refused to deliver judgment where proof was, he said, impossible.

His decision to forsake the forest life horrified his still orthodox disciples, who forsook him, probably fearing a cruel martyrdom at Banāras. Buddha, however, hesitated not, but wended his lone way, and encamped by the sacred *kund* or well of Sār-nāth, two or three miles N.E. of the city.

Here it was he opened the campaign—one brave man against the surrounding millions, who clung to their ancient superstitions.

What had he to offer in opposition to the wishes of all these nations? Naught, than simple *Common-sense*, or, as he named it, "Right Doing and Right Thinking"; that which Buddhists called *Dharma* and *Bhāva Chakra*, "The Wheel of the Law"—the Evolution of *Bhāvana* or Existence.

Within half a century—the Hindu Rome—Banāras itself, and great kings and peoples, owned his reasonable, kindly sway; and before he had passed away (or, as they said, "attained *Nirvāna*"), many millions worshiped the very ground wherever his weary steps had trodden, and hailed him as the only one who had ever brought home to them enlightenment and peace, such as they had never before experienced.

BUDDHA'S CREED IN HIS EARLY JAINA STAGE.

I

Come unto me all ye who are bowed down
With the sorrows and evils of a weary life
And I will show unto you the way of peace.*
Remember that the flesh ever tries to rule the spirit,
Set therefore before thee good laws and precepts.
Begin by controlling the body by a strict regimen,
Abstaining from rich foods, and eating only at stated periods.
Art thou young ? shun dances, songs, and gaieties,
For they corrupt the heart, and make thee frivolous ;
Avoid ornaments, perfumes and soft couches,
And touch not money—the root of most evils.

II

The good man obeys the following primary laws :
I. He covets nought which is another's, nor touches it.
II. He drinks not, nor associates with a drunkard.
III. He speaks no falsehood, be it to save his life.
IV. He neither destroys nor injures the life of animal or insect,
V. And looks not on another woman than his wife.

III

Wouldst thou excel in righteousness ?
Then part with all thou hast and wear
The rags which others have cast away.
Live but on alms, and take one meal daily ;
Reside in solitary places apart from men,

---

* The sage's words were : "Draw nigh unto me ye wounded ones, afflicted and distressed, and I will fold you in my arms. My religion is a path wide as the heavens, where the highest and lowest caste, rich and poor, old and young, can walk and dwell together."

And seek only their haunts for thy morning alms.
Let the trunk of the tree be thy pillow,
And only its foliage thy garment of sleep.
    Take no thought for the morrow,
    But amid the tombstones of men
    Do thou nightly meditate
On the transitoriness of all human things.

GOTAMA'S SECOND OR TRUE BUDDHIST STAGE ON LEAVING GAYĀ

I

Be up and doing, work for the good of all mankind,
Regarding not thine own comfort, or salvation.
Put away covetousness, self-seeking and sloth;
Be energetic in mind and body, but meek in heart and word;
Seek contemplation, so that thou mayest be full of wisdom,
And seek learning in order to know and practise every virtue.
Entertain no evil desires, nor think wrong of any one,
Modestly regard thyself, and be fearful of sinning.
Persevere in goodness however thou mayest be opposed,
And forgive injuries however oft persisted in.

II

Be willing to receive, and profit by reproof;
Have contentment and gratitude with sympathy for all;
Moderation in prosperity, submission in affliction
And cheerfulness at all times.
He who can act thus will enjoy the perfection of happiness,
And perhaps hereafter supreme reward.

III

Yet, having done all, count not thyself good,
Nor seek a return, even in personal happiness;
Virtue indeed has its own reward here and hereafter,
But beware lest thou seek this in rites and ceremonies;
For that is no true virtue which seeketh reward,
Which crieth "Give and it shall be given unto thee,"
But that which, uninfluenced by any creed or faith
Or hopes or fears, giveth, expecting no return.

IV

He truly is divine who is pure in heart and life,
Fearing only that he does not sufficiently show this
By unselfish actions, sympathy, and kind words
And full faith in the regeneration of his race.

V

Not by birth art thou lowered, nor by birth does the
Wise man esteem thee, but by thy words and deeds
Dost thou fall and rise in his just estimation.
Folly and ignorance is common among all ranks,
Yea, the ascetic's garb oft covers the irreligious mind
As does a humble as well as lordly guise, a celestial heart.

VI

Encourage learning everywhere and at all times, for
Ignorance is the chief cause of evils and superstitions.
Knowledge is the only wealth which thieves cannot steal,
And by zeal and diligence it can be garnered everywhere;
But as music cometh only by playing on instruments,
So seek the company of, and ponder the words of the wise.
Indolence soon defiles young and old. Hold high the torch
And busy thyself in works of usefulness and mercy.

VII

Nought is so precious as the first steps to holiness,
Nor so attractive and useful to all mankind;
Therefore specially cherish youthful efforts to goodness,
They oft recur in later years when evil temptations wax strong.

VIII

It is Nature's rule, that as we sow, we shall reap,
She recognises no good intentions, and pardons no errors;
Therefore no deeds, virtuous or sinful, are to us of
Small importance. All must bear some fruit
And must follow us like shadows for good or ill,
Mayhap to rankle secretly and for ever to poison our lives.

IX

Begin by restraining and conquering thyself;
Practise the art of "Giving up"—of doing unto all
As thou wouldst have them do unto thee.
Weary not in well-doing, but be active and earnest,
Sympathetic and benevolent even in thy thoughts
Concerning others, and courteous in words and manner.
Guard well thy thoughts for they determine what thou
Art towards others, as well as thy innermost spirit.

X

Observe "the old rule" that soft words and looks dissipate anger.
Return good for evil, justice for injustice;
Remembering that hatred is only overcome by love;
That as evil develops evil, so does good, goodness,
And that righteousness yields happiness unto the doer.
Seek not thus however, any personal boon or advantage
But only the highest good of all sentient creatures.

XI

Virtuous conduct comes naturally to him who practises virtue,
And his heart and life will be full with kindly activities—
With the spirit of charity, gentleness, purity and truth;
Let these be precious to thee as the breath of life.

XII

Believe not all ye hear, nor all traditions, however sacred;
Nor though handed down through many generations,
Believed by millions, and repeated by the good and wise—
Thy respected teachers and most revered elders.
All are liable to err and to believe mere conjectures,
And especially what cometh to us by birth and habit.

XIII

Seek a reason for all things; analize, investigate and see
If the subject be one tending to the general welfare:
Only then accept it, and live up to thy convictions.*

XIV

"To cease from sin, attain virtue and a pure heart
Is the religion of Buddhas," not rites and ceremonies;
Not reading of Vedas, shaving the head or going naked
In dirt or rough garments; no penances nor any
Prayers or sacrifices here availeth or cleanseth thee.

XV

An angry nature, evil words, envy, hatred and malice
Defileth more than the eating of forbidden flesh.
Sin can only be atoned by ceasing to sin;
No priest can gain for thee or grant to thee salvation,
And sacrifices but injure the innocent, are cruel and selfish.
Thou mayst not seek good by doing an evil deed,
And to inflict injury on any sentient creature is a
Breach of all the laws of just and moral conduct.

* *cf. Kalama Sutta* in M. Muller's *Vedānta*, p. 114.

XVI

Maintain the body in vigorous health if thou
Wouldst aid in good works and fellowship, for
Self-mortification and toil is not progress ;
It is the teaching of heretics and the slothful.

XVII

The best penance is patient and silent long sufferance ;
The best good, righteous desires and a chaste spirit ;
Temperance in all things ; pleasant speech ;
Good words spoken in love and in due season :*
The knowledge of noble truths and a mind
Which trembles not under worldly afflictions,
These are treasures too little valued and practised.

XVIII

If thou wouldst have mercy, be just and merciful ;
Sympathise with sorrow, and rejoice with the joyful,
Ever striving to fill the world with loving-kindness.
Till well thine own field, and help others to do likewise ;
And accept no exaltation to the prejudice of another.

XIX

Cultivate equanimity and patience under all conditions ;
Life is full of sorrows. They are part of Nature's order,
Which the wise man accepts as inevitable,
But does his best to alleviate and utilize.
With this view he may seek for long life, power, and health,
And this even for those who desire to follow in his steps,
So that wrongs and miseries may be thus mitigated.

---

* *cf.* Paul's ἀληθεύων ἐν ἀγάπῃ and πλήρωμα νόμου ἡ ἀγάπη; and *I. Tsing's Buddhist Religion* in India in 680. Takakusu's trans., 1896.

XX

Nature gives blow for blow, not good for evil;
Yet the wildest animals are overcome by kindness;
The liar, by truths; and the illiberal by generosity.
Victory breeds hatred, and victors are ill at ease;
He is the greatest conqueror, who controls himself,
And unselfishness is the surest path to peace;
But be tranquil, and heedless of victory or defeat.

XXI

Think lightly of no sin, lest it overtake thee;
Be vigilant, for only the well trained mind is secure:
The diligent one who fears sloth cannot fall away.
Meditation or *Dhāyna* will give thee wisdom;
And who so perseveres in this is nigh unto Nirvăna.

XXII

Live up to thine own teachings and the highest knowledge;
Be earnest though others are heedless, and scrutinize them
Only to correct thine own shortcomings, for all fall short,
Neglecting what they should do, and doing what they should avoid.

XXIII

Be ever more ready to praise than to blame any,
For the fault-finder has need to be himself faultless;
Yet withstand the wrong-doer and the evil speaker,
Instructing with judgment if they will hearken.
Perchance ignorance, error, or a wrong have misled,
And by enlightening thou mayest guide aright.

XXIV

Be long suffering, meek, pious, and tranquil;
Practise and accept what is good in all teachings;
Fine words without good actions are fruitless,
And beguile alike the teacher and the taught.
Reason out thy faith earnestly and with simplicity,
Submitting all to reason, thy surest guide amidst
The fallacies and sophisms of creeds and philosophies.

XXV

Love and venerate thy parents, and respect the aged;
Help the young, the bereaved, the sick, and helpless.
Take thought for thy friend, and fear to offend him.
Let husbands love their wives, and wives revere their husbands.
Judge none hastily, harshly, or by outward appearances,
But calmly and sympathetically, remembering that thou
Too are far from having attained to the "Perfect Way."

XXVI

Thou must work to live, but chose a peaceful calling;
And give of thy earnings to the virtuous needy.
Live righteously, doing as thou wouldst be done by;
Nor let ingratitude weary thee in well doing.
Subdue thyself, if thou desirest to subdue others,
And the former is a yet harder task than the latter.

XXVII

Go forth, and *alone*, into all lands and preach holiness;
Trusting in its serene power, and in no arm of flesh.
Instruct rich and poor, males and females, priests and peoples,
Driving away ignorance, and befriending the wronged.
Let thy words be as lotuses, rich in scent and in colour,
Springing from the depths of a pure heart and mind.

XXVIII

Decry not other sects, faiths, or individuals,
But accept truth under whatever garb it may appear:
Rendering due honour unto whom honour is due.

XXIX

Doubts and difficulties must exist whilst minds endure,
They are agents and progressive forces of man's nature,
And must not hinder us in the pursuits of virtue
However rugged and difficult they make the path.

XXX

Busy not yourselves anxiously and unprofitably
About other worlds, gods, souls, spirits or demons;
Of thy coming hither and from whence; of the soul's existence,
And if it be, of its going hence, when and unto where?
Nought is proven; all this is unknown and unknowable,
Whilst the duties of life are substantial and urgent.

XXXI

I have preached the truth, withholding naught,
Nor recognising aught which others call esoteric.
To teach of souls or mysteries, or of a life hereafter,
Is a misleading and barren speculation for the masses;
It leads them away from facts, which it usually distorts,
And from duties and studies, immediate and imperative.

XXXII

Let us strive for Nirvāna or perfection even here,
By driving out all delusions, ignorance and stupidity;
This is to turn aright the "Wheel of Law" and *Dharma*,
Whilst craving after a future life is weakness and folly.

XXXIII

Let us break the many fetters which bind us to Self;
Striving after *Sotāpanno* or Conversion of the heart—
The development of goodness and pious habits,
The destruction of all selfish delusions;
And of *Kāma* or that evil spirit of sensuality
Which all ethics and religions alike condemn.

XXXIV

Askest thou of Brāhma—the Spirit of the Universe?
Such is incomprehensible, infinite, emotionless;
Therefore weary not thyself, seeking after the hidden:
Work: for the paths of duty lie close before thee,
Behold thy brethren call unto thee from the ground,
From miseries, perplexing and unspeakable,
Which, if thou wouldst, thou couldst alleviate.

XXXV

"Trouble not yourselves because I pass away;"
It is of the nature of things that all must separate;
For "whatsoever exists is without endurance,"
And death may be only a beginning of new life:
By it we may live in the assemblies which follow—
Mayhap "in the foundation of a Kingdom of Righteousness."

XXXVI

Ye, my disciples, have run well; continue to be
Earnest in the duties of life, vigilant unto the end;
So will ye reach unto supreme wisdom,
"An unconditional state—the fruition of enlightenment."

PINDAR

FL. 512 B.C. (552-442)

Think not thou to escape condemnation
Who now revelest in all wickedness;
As the just shall go to rest and joy,
So surely shalt thou to a just reward
In a world of misery, though mayhap not eternal.

The Supreme delighteth not in troubling thee,
But rather that thou be righteous and enjoy thy life here,
And live thereafter with the gods, beloved and honored;
Yea, in "a heaven for ever bright by day and night,
  Exulting in a flood of light;
  From labor free and all distress,
  The great abode of happiness."

CONFUCIUS, or KHUNG-FU-TSZE

FL. 510 B.C. (551-478)

Short Texts gleaned from accounts of his life, his *Classics* and *Discourses*, thus forming

THE CONFUCIAN BIBLE OF THE SIXTH CENT. B.C.

I

He who desires to establish a nation securely
Must educate the young and diffuse intelligence;
An ignorant people can neither be healthy,
Orderly, good, contented or peaceable;
Nor a firm and good king be esteemed a kindly ruler.

II

The parent is the base of the national system
And must inculcate virtue, loyalty and patriotism.
The king crowns the edifice as "father of the people,"
And he should excel in all virtues, and in his rule
Temper justice with mercy, love and sympathy.
He is the chief servant—the enthroned guardian of the state,
And should consider the achievement of justice
His all-sufficient profit; and the prosperity and happiness
Of the nation as his best and enduring reward.

III

A ruler or father who neglects his duties
Is as much to blame as the disloyal and unfilial son;
Therefore in punishing him, neglect not the prime offender
Who ought to have better brought up his household.

IV

Evil is not inherent in our human nature;
The babe is innocent and even prone to virtue:
It is circumstances, violence and vicious surroundings
That beget like conduct and inclinations.

V

We are the resultant forces of "the Heavens" and Earth;
The male and female principles of nature,
An eflux from the eternal source of law and order,
To whom virtue has an irresistible charm;
And virtues will not stand alone,
But ever seek out and find many neighbors.

VI

Nature or "TÏ-EN is the supreme idea of law and order."
It betokens intelligence, and is worshiped as *Shang Ti*.
We are but puny "parts of a stupendous mechanism,"
Which is " self-sustaining and without beginning or end."

VII

We can but see and study the laws of cause and effect ;
But of *Creation* we can know nought, only *Expansion*.
Our knowledge is bounded by the phenomenal ;
That which can be comprehended by our senses,
Cultured by experiences, reason and thought,
And carefully stored up in our memories.

VIII

Discuss therefore phenomena, and the laws of Nature,
And waste not time on the vain speculations of religions ;
As on primeval and final causes, creation and its end,
Primordial Matter and Spirit, Gods, Life and Souls,
Time and space, infinity, immortality, heavens and hells.

IX

Knowing so little of this life, and what life is,
How canst thou comprehend death and the Beyond ?
All except the teachings of experience and reflection
Is to us unknown, and perchance ever unknowable ;
Be here therefore silent, neither opposing nor supporting.
Even the divinations of sorcerers may come true ;
And having a hold on the ignorant and imaginative,
Should be respected though not countenanced.

X

Sufficient for our ordinary powers and activities
Are the varied and well known phenomena of nature.
Be content if thou understand the visible and palpable,
And can execute well thy homely and social duties.
These are prominent and never hid as is the
Whither, Whence and Wherefore of life.

XI

He who wishes to fulfil the highest purposes of life
Should begin by ordering well his own house and conduct;
Thus best will he aid and inspire the life of the future.
If unable to influence his fellows and the known,
How can he influence the unknown and the "heavens"?
But by acting rightly man masters his own destiny,
Aids and guides the feeble, ignorant, and wavering;
And himself has nought to fear concerning the unknown.

XII

The future is impenetrable; no gods have spoken; no dead arisen,
Whilst Nature has ever moved on unconcernedly
And in eternal silence, producing and disintegrating;
Calous apparently of the feelings, joys, or miseries of all creation.
And crushing relentlessly all who oppose her ways.

XIII

Thus are our paths full of dangerous perplexities,
And give full scope for foresight and all virtues.
Goodness is as a rule the produce of intellectuality,
And vice the offspring of ignorance; but e'en wisdom
Oft times halts in the paths of rectitude and virtue.
Nevertheless seek after learning, individual and national,
And esteem wisdom above all treasures, wealth, and power.

XIV

If thou really desirest and would bravely find knowledge,
Open thine ears willingly to all men's views;
Have ability to study and comprehend their scope,
And the will, courage and honesty to follow truth at all
Times, and however at first distasteful and unpopular.

XV

The good and wise man is calm, tolerant, and no partizan;
The ignorant man hasty, ungenerous, and not catholik.
He acts best who unselfishly, with piety and purity,
Strives to be true to his best and highest instincts;
And holds up to himself the highest aims and ideals.
This path leads to no priest or temple, but to the gates of heaven—
The highest satisfaction of the heart and mind, and yields
That inward reward which belongeth only to the good and true.

XVI

Good deeds as well as vices follow after us,
And live in our children to several generations.
Nature's moral laws are as stern as her physical;
So if thou hast been foolish in the past,
Bemoan it not; she never overlooks or forgives;
The past is gone, and for thee is irrevocable;
Bestir thyself afresh, and be wiser in the future.

XVII

The world needs workers, not monks and anchorites—
Mistaken pietists, who in forsaking their fellows,
Identify themselves with the animal creation.
Our duties demand that we live with and for mankind,
Playing well our part, alike by example and by precept.

XVIII

Help with diligence the oppressed, the weak and ignorant
According to thy full capabilities and influence.
Be brave, manly, sincere, modest and generous,
And if thou wouldst rule others, learn first
To rule thine own thoughts, words and actions.

XIX

Exercise economy, and restrict thine own pleasures,
So that seeing thee, the mean man may become
Liberal, and the selfish and miserly bountiful.
Admonish loyally and kindly even thy friend,
Yet pause if thou find him angry or impracticable.

XX

Instruct high and low to honor their parents and superiors,
To sympathize with and help their neighbors.
Oppose oppression, all wrongs and injustice
With firmness, yet without violence or anger.

XXI

Treat the aged with deference, if not reverence,
And disturb not the serenity of their lives.
The wisest and strongest will become weak and foolish,
Withering away like the leaves of the forest.
Honor thou their memories with befitting tombs
And rites as prescribed by our ancestors.

XXII

If thou art a teacher, consider well thy high calling,
And lend not the weight of thy name to foolish theories—
Those speculations which unlearned ones are prone to.
It is thy duty to curb, teach and direct men aright,
So that they waste not their substance, time and abilities.

XXIII

Knowledge is only that which you know accurately.
Whatsoever you have not fully and clearly mastered,
Consider you do not know, and refrain from teaching.
Frankly confess the limits of your knowledge;
To know that you do not know, is the beginning of wisdom.

XXIV

Not more surely does grass bend before the wind
Than the masses to the will and example of leaders;
Therefore think out well what thou wouldst teach,
And beware of unlearned meditation;
For undigested studies can be of use to none,
And thought unassisted by learning is perilous.

XXV

Neither as ruler nor citizen turn thy cheek to the smiter.
Recompence injury with justice, not kindness;
Else wilt thou recompence evil doers and establish
Laws which would disintegrate society.
The Law of "*Reciprocity*" and the "foundation of order" is:
"Do unto another what you would he did unto you;
And do not that which you would not have done to yourself."

XXVI

Weigh well the difficulties which surround thy path,
Then shall no difficulty overcome thee.
There is a bravery which surpasses that of
The soldier, the huntsman, and the mariner.
To be brave under every trial of life, small or great,
Even if the heavens seem against us;
Acting well our part with stalwart will,
And bearing our burdens with cheerful hearts.

XENOPHANES.

Founder of Eleatik School.   Fl. 495   (535-445 b.c.)

I

Have I not upheld the oneness of the universe,
And of God, the one and the self-existent?
Let us be faithful to our varied convictions,
Yet open to every fresh gleam of light and truth.
Though we know somewhat of truth and perfection,
Yet error is spread amidst all things.

II

The cherished convictions of my youth
Maturer years and research have condemned,
Still will I proclaim all known truths,
And diligently search for more.
The *certain* and the *absolute* in truth
Man may never attain unto,
Yet the greater the diligence in search,
The greater will be our reward.

III

Away with the gods of a Homer and a Hesiod,
Whose broken promises, lusts, and deceits
Proclaim them but the ideas of men like unto themselves.
The Zeus of the Ethiopians has a flat nose and a black skin,
But the Thrakian loves his blue eyed and ruddy-hued god.

IV

A personal god is abhorent to me,
For it recalls to my mind all that I myself am—
A being grovelling and finite, having passions,
Respirations and excretions.

V

Ex nihilo, nihil fit—out of nothing, nothing comes ;
God is all, He is Existent Being, and embracing all existence.
My god is of all things human and divine, *the* perfection,
Neither like mortal in body nor in spirit :
He is one, the unchangeable, the immovable,
The infinite vault, the perfect sphere ;
The incomprehensible, the unnameable—
The bosom on which many move. By wisdom and foreknowledge
He ruleth all, and wearieth not nor slumbereth.

HERAKLEITOS, "The Weeping Philosopher"
FL. 495 B.C. (535-475)

I

All is, yet all is not, even thought but breathes and dies.
Yet the earth was, is, and shall be, for it is developed heat.
Primeval water was but a phaze of eternal, sacred fire,
"The self-kindled and self-extinguished," from which all evolved,
"Not made by God or man, but the growth of immutable law,
By which too comes the soul—the god-like part of a rational whole.

II

Mortal men strangely crave for the immortality of the gods,
Though none have ever sailed twice even on the same stream.
Though we embark, we embark not, we are and are not.
Contentment is the one Goal we should all strive after—
"A perfect acquiescence" in the decrees of supreme law.

III

Be still and learn from God, as the child waiteth on his master.
Trust not your own knowledge nor senses, which are deceitful.

IV

All is subject to fate, though ordered by reason and intelligence;
The senses are a poor aid to unravel creative mysteries.
Death awaiteth us all—the just and the unjust;
Yet is there a future which man has not conceived of,
And which the most righteous dare scarce hope for?

V

Our God is one, the ever restless changing force of all things;
That universal motion which lives, fades, and grows again;
Out of endless strife he deduces perfect harmony,
As music springs from the smitten lyre.

'ASKLÉPIOS

FL. 485 B.C. (525-456)

Dread Jove rules and formed us, as the potter the clay,
And we seem but the sport of superior powers.
We can but resign ourselves to an irrevocable destiny,
Consoled by the hope of retributive compensation.

Jove teaches wisdom by sins, which bring with them remorse,
And thus induces good even through a surfeit of evil.
Yet to the wise man Heaven imparts strength,
And whoso is just, shall at last go scathless.

PARMÉNIDES

FL. 486 B.C. (520-450)

Reason says nought exists save one great Being,
Sensuous impression says, many things and beings;
But truth is the pure child of reason,
Whilst opinions and ideas belong but to sense.

The knowledge of physics may be delusive,
But mathematics teach truths eternal and self-evident.
Thoughts are but children of a moment,
Subject to every breeze and circumstance.
God, the one, is all existence, identical and unique,
Neither born nor dying, moving nor changing.

ANAXĀGORAS

FL. 460 B.C. (500-420)

I

Supreme intelligence regulates all the universe,
As must reason all our various faculties.
Thy senses can see *Phainomena* but not *Noumena*.
It requires reason to separate substance from appearance.

II

Thou perceivest a mass and callest it a flower,
Go ask reason to verify and control this impression.
Nothing can come of nothing; gold was ever gold,
And blood, blood, but the Harmonizer can mix them.
Thou sayest " God created and ordained all things ;
How knowest thou then that fire burnt thee " ?

III

All is good and there is nothing unintelligent
Nor conflicting in the phenomena of nature.
Nothing comes into being nor is destroyed,
All is an aggregation or segregation of that which was.
Creation is but a commingling of things which are,
And corruption their separation and remingling.

IV

That which to thy finite vision was indistinguishable,
Was still there " in infinite number and smallness,"
Perhaps being sorted into " noticeable quality,"
But still atoms—arranging under the Supreme Intellect.

V

Thou art but a product of the materials thou consumest,
And originally sprang from humid earth warmed by sunlight.
Thy materiality is ever at enmity with things spiritual,
And with but a short life, weakly intellect and limited senses,
Remember that thou canst comprehend and learn little,
And can never attain unto certainty in anything.—

VI

I say not with some that "The Great All" is one,
Rather that He is many and the harmonizer of all.
He is the incorporeal, immaterial and evanescent *Nous*
Which penetrates and energizes the universe;
We call Him not a *Creator* but a great *Former*,
Who but moulded the pre-existent.

N.B.—For such teaching the pious philosopher was condemned by the Athenians for blasphemy; saying that he dethroned Apollo by referring phenomena to natural laws, and by speaking of the sun and moon as but earths with soils and stones; and the great statesman Perikles nearly shared the same judgment. The Persian Mazdeans seized and imprisoned Anaxagoras, and condemned him to death for teaching what Magians considered a heresy—the antagonism of mind and matter; but he escaped through Perikles and died in exile and poverty—a good and genuine martyr.

PERIKLES
FL. 460 (B.C. —?-429)

The universe is governed by law, order and intelligence,
Which seek thou to understand through phenomena.
Guard well thy words that they be not inappropriate
To thy cause, unjust or even irritating to any.
Keep thy heart pure and thy hands clean,
And let not thine eyes dwell on iniquity.

SOPHOKLES
FL. 456 (B.C. 496-405)

No power of man can check thy might, O Zeus,
Thou art "The One" who sleepest not, nor waxeth faint;
The maker of heavens and earth—controller of winds and waters,
No ordinance of ours can override thy laws,
Which from age to age and everywhere endureth.

Thou abhorrest evil and all who act wickedly;
And lovest those who are the pure and good;
Making them doubly blessed at the gates of death
What time the wicked suffer for their sin.

ZENO OF ELEA
FL. 450 (B.C. 490-— ?)

God is absolute intelligence, foreseeing and thinking;
He is all powerful and like unto the sphere—complete;
But incorporeal, mysterious and incomprehensible;
The immovable, original and originator of all things;
The supreme, the best and only Lord God;
The essence of fire and heat, and generator of all life.

EMPÊDOKLÊS

FL. 450 (490-430 B.C.)

I

From earth, fire, air and water—the four primitives,
Sprang all things, and by like we know like.
Heat proclaims fire, as does strife, hate ; and love, love.

II

Man is an outcast from the gods, ever striving and unsubmissive ;
Better that he offer cakes and incense to the Queen of Heaven ;
And strive to master his own evil passions.

III

The wise trust not sensations or feelings but *Reason* ;
Though our emotional nature oft clouds its divinity.
Whoso liveth wisely and morally, helps himself and the state ;
For ignorance is the chief source of our ills and even epidemics.
These neither come nor go miraculously, but are
Caused by negligence, filth, noxious air, water or moisture.

IV

Seek for reasons and causes : out of nothing, nothing comes ;
Nor can the existing ever pass into non-existence.
Out of a laboratory replete with original elements,
Nature mixes and separates, unalterable substances.
Motion we call life, but tranquility is not death,
Nor is this change any annihilation of matter.

V

Nature's two great powers are attraction and repulsion,
Originally reposeful in one conceivable divine *sphairos*—
A sphere in which rested the divine universal mind—
Ineffably holy, swift-glancing, all-pervading thought
And love; the Eternal Cause and Necessity of all things—
Visible in Phenomena, but to our senses incomprehensible.

PROTAGORAS

"The Logos and First Sophist."   Fl. 452 b.c. (482-411)

I

If thou wouldst have the world progress in healthy happiness,
Then educate all and strive to induce cultured thought
Rather than physical research and the technical.
If the house be well governed, so will be the state.

II

Herakleitos well saith : All is motion, active or passive,
Hence our sensations or perceptions, color, sound and sight—
Ever varying according to the velocity of motion.

III

Everything is perpetually *becoming*; nothing *is*.
We conceive or perceive through the eternal
Ever changing but rhythmic motion of matter,
So that our sensations like their objects, move also.

IV

There exists for each of us, only what we have sensations of;
For only what the individual sensates, can be to him existent.
Hence "man is to man the measure of all things";
And he may justifiably rest on his perceptions.

V

But the percipient may be defective in sensations,
And must therefore strive to attain higher activities,
Clearer perceptions and deeper knowledge of phenomena,
And of the extension of matter in time and space.

VI

"Of the gods, I am incapable of asserting that they exist
Or do not exist," or of any future or eternal world.
That which is absolute, self-existent and unconditioned,
Must be to us, mayhap for ever, a *beyond* or mere *idea*.

VII

Seek pleasure in the good and beautiful; in all the virtues,
And in holiness of thought and life, but especially
In the duties of thy station which affect others.
Continue to educate thyself, resting not in a quiescent
Conviction of knowledge nor of the insufficiency thereof.

VIII

Though the absolute in truth be unattainable,
Be practical; for society must hold some opinions;
And it is the duty of the wise to form and guide these,
Adapting them to the wants and exigencies of the times,
And the circumstances and culture of the people.

EURIPIDĒS

FL. 441 (480-406 B.C.)

None know the beginning of time or of all things,
Yet say we: "Nought that e'er has been, completely dies;
That things combined before, another union find,
Quitting the old, they in other forms appear."

'Twere best not to reason upon or investigate
The mysteries of religions and mythologies,
But to accept those handed down to us.
Interpret these so that thine own God be just and benevolent,
One slow to anger, who correcteth the proud,
The wicked, and those who despise holiness.

All is mystery, none can truly describe Zeus;
Vaguely they call Him " Providence, Nature, Intelligence "—
Words which but confuse and darken counsel.
He is a noiseless, unseen, but all-pervading Power.
I posit him as all-mighty, just, good, and merciful;
One hating iniquity, yet mysteriously permitting it.
And I pray to him, believing he will hear me.

GORGIAS

FL. 440 (B.C. 480-375)

Nought has any existence or reality, only appearance,
If more than this, it is beyond our power to ascertain it,
Or to communicate it; else would it be real and knowable.

If existence were known, then thought were existence,
The non-existent must for ever remain unthinkable.
" Things neither *are*, nor *are not*, otherwise
Being and *non-being* would be identical."

The *Senses* do not prove that anything exists;
Words can but show corresponding perceptions,
And are only intelligible approximately;
No two persons having like perceptions and sentiments.

SOKRATES

FL. 430 (B.C. 469-399)

I

I have learned this much, that I know nothing,
But I can investigate and show what is false.
Remember thou that it is the wise man's chief duties
Not only to know what he knows, but what he knows not.

II

My life has been devoted to teaching and talking with men,
I have neither written, lectured, nor sought for reward,
The phenomena of mind, not nature, have been my theme;
Though no sophist, I have ever discoursed on morals.

III

Sensuous impressions are indeed swift and deceptive,
Yet not so the decisions of a good man's conscience.
The soul, and not sacrifices, is God's delight,
And all can offer to him their meed of duty and love.

IV

Many indeed bear the thyrsus, thus professing their faith,
But few possess the spirit which it demands.
Let virtue be the supreme rule of thy life,
And look that thou severely adhere to righteousness.

V

God though ever invisible is omnipresent,
Supreme in power, wisdom and foreknowledge.
Man has only seen his all-governing spirit
Through the phenomena of his universe;
Yet he secretly pervades all, and is the moving spirit
By which thou hast life, and laws governing all wisely.

VI

Ascribe not thy successes to thine own wisdom
But to a right appreciation of the wise laws of Zeus;
Seek from him all high and spiritual gifts,
Not knowledge which thou can'st acquire for thyself.

VII

He is Sophia, reason, wisdom and goodness,
And the author only of all that is good.
Seeing, then, there is law, order and design everywhere,
That each creation is fitted for its own mode of life,
Why doubtest thou of the Lawgiver and Designer,
And talkest ignorantly of blind force, or chance?

VIII

Have the gods taken no thought of thee
That they have given to thee a soul above the beasts?
An attribute without which thou know'st not of Zeus.
Believe then, and acknowledge that the good and pious
Are also renowned for wisdom and good fortune.

IX

As thy soul resides in and governs the body,
So the universal soul pervades and rules the world;
As thine eye sees all near and far, great and small,
How much more does deity comprehend all?

X

Fear no man, nay, welcome the martyr's crown,
For to a guiltless soul it is a glad reward.
It is for rulers to fear the echoes of the martyr's knell,
But the good man fears only guilt, not death.
The foolish king beheading the wise, seeketh peace,
But the wise ruler seeketh conviction and excellence.
Death to me and the faithful man is but new birth—
A step to a far higher and better state of being.

DEMOKRITOS OF ABDERA

"The Laughing Philosopher"

fl. 428 (b.c. 465-375)

I

Nothing is true, or if so, it is unknown to us;
We know not even if there is anything to know.
For only through our senses come our thoughts,
And these are but subjectively, not objectively true.
We know sweet from bitter, but truth only by reflexion.

II

By our senses can come experiences, and hence
Intelligence, knowledge, and mental power;
But the senses are liable to error from many causes.

III

All things are composed of invisible, intangible,
And indivisible *atoms*, variously combining;
And these exist everywhere except in vacuum.
They are extended, infinitely minute, ponderable,
Impenetrable, uncaused, and eternal.

IV

They vary in shape and density, and are ever in motion,
And have variable affinities called attraction and repulsion—
Powers by which the world is formed and moves;
For by the inhaling and exhaling of these, all life
Is maintained, or as we say perishes or dies.

V

New things are but a varied aggregation of atoms,
Even the soul, breath or life, is but a fire atom
Which attains to perception and knowledge by slow ignition
Through the warmth of its corporeal environment.
It dies or "is not," when separated therefrom, and
Like fire, it is unknown and exists not in a vacuum,
And its powers alter according to circumstances.

VI

The popular mythologies point to beings with powers
Higher than man, who may influence human
Affairs either malevolently or benevolently.

VII

Let *Euthumia* be the ultimate object of all our actions,
For "freedom from care" and passion is philosophy's best fruit;
Attempt not therefore that which is beyond thy powers,
And so be free from the griefs of the unsuccessful.

VIII

Be not cast down by adversity, nor elated by prosperity,
But find true joy in mental activity, and a good conscience
Begotten by just and benevolent acts, extended even
If possible unto all mankind.

ISOKRATES

FL. 395 (436-338 B.C.)

"Be assured, O King Salamis,
That the most grateful adoration and sacrifice
Thou canst render to God is to give him thy heart"—
By doing good, thinking good and administering justice.
Act to all as thou desirest they should act towards thee.

PLATO

FL. 390 (B.C. 428-347)

I

Add to true piety goodness in heart and life,
And seek ever to dwell in spirit with thy God.
His Word or Logos ever dwelleth in our midst,
And from eternity He was and ever shall be.

II

All true knowledge and wisdom cometh from God,
And to attain these is the highest aim of the philosopher.
Search thou for them as others seek for earthly treasures,
For they will purify thy soul and through thee, others.

III

God, the Unconditioned, Absolute and Unrestricted ruleth all,
And evil and suffering are modes of his wisdom, which
Man cannot now understand or see reason for.
He may yet do so when to the divine Creative idea, he adds
A knowledge of all the material of phenomena,
That which encompasseth both mind and matter.

IV

Physiologists can at present only attain unto probabilities,
For physics treat only of the changeable and imitative;
The spiritual deals with the soul of the universe—
That which is of the same nature as our souls,
Our immaterial and immortal ego or psychê,
Part of the divine essence which corresponds to
And can communicate with the Eternal Logos.

V

Through many transmigrations, pains, trials and sorrows
Has thy soul reached thee, and through yet more
Must it pass ere attaining to perfection,
For thus only can its sins be expurgated.
It is not without memories of the past,
Nay unites our past and present, and appetite with spirit.

VI

The soul is one of an invariable and constant number,
It has a faculty of reason which is God-like and sublime;
The whole body exists but for its development.
By it thou differest from the brute, recollecting
And reasoning, making thy past, part of thy present.

VII

From reasonable and necessary *a priori* truths,
Man can discover and analyze the mysteries of life;
But it is not given him to know all phenomenal facts,
And synthetically to attain unto perfect wisdom.

VIII

From primitive ideas however, man may soar aloft
Over a gross and mundane materialism,
But must walk warily, and dialectically mature knowledge,
If he would deal with such abstract subtleties.

IX

Cultivate a love which transcends sensual weakness,
And link thy intellectual being with the beautiful and eternal;
With the moral purity which appertains to thy soul—
That spirit which ever was, and must remain, untainted.

X

Seek after true goodness, for this is never injurious;
It is to be found only by wide and thoughtful knowledge.
True pleasure is the maintenance of true harmony;
Pain and misery, but disturbance and discordance.

XI

Virtue is the development of the highest good;
It is the science and practice of perfect righteousness.
Virtue fits the soul for the operations peculiar to it,
But much wisdom is necessary to attain to virtue.

XII

We have a trinity of principles in "God, Matter, and Ideas,"
Yet Zeus is a personal and independent entity
Who intellectually moulds matter—"the mother of forms,"
But which is nevertheless a refractory, resisting mass.

XIII

There is no evil in the appointments of the gods,
Nor in those of Nature—"parent of all things."
Nought comes by blind chance, but all has
Been foreordained, so that struggling through the
Present life, we may have joys in eternity.

XIV

He who cares least for his bodily nature,
Striving to remain pure till God releases him,
Approaches nearest to him—"The Absolute One,"
And to that purity without which we cannot see him.

XV

That which cometh as a necessity to all men
Cannot be evil to any just one,
For the whole, as well as each part, is perfect,
And ministered over by a presiding spirit.

XVI

Each creation is for the sake of the whole,
Which exists also but to benefit each part.
Thou too art part of the great whole,
And that which is best for thee is also
Best for each portion of the universe.

XVII

Zeus is the measure of all things,
And to be dear to him strive to be like him.
Seek converse with him in prayer, and in
Every service which conduces to this end.

XVIII

As a citizen, merge thy life in the service of the state,
And, ignoring thyself, be governed by the wisest.
Give not, however, unlimited power to any man,
But reconcile freedom with reason and unity;
Mingle monarchy with popular democracy,
And acknowledge capacity wherever found.

DIOGENES OF APOLLONIA
FL. 370 (412-323 B.C.)

I say not, with Thales, that water is the *Arché*,
But, with Anaximander, that this is air;
For is not breath the vital energy of all nature,
Yea, of man's own soul and intelligence?
Yet does the soul surpass its author or former,
And air and soul cannot exist apart.*

---

* Here the term *Soul* is as closely recognized as *Breath*, as in Hebrew *Ruh* and *Napash;* the Indian terms *Atman* and *Jiva* (Life-breath); Greek *animos psyché* and *pneuma*, and our *spirit* as based on *spiro*.

SHORT TEXTS IN FAITHS AND PHILOSOPHIES.

ARISTOTLE, The Stagyrite
fl. 345 (b.c. 384-322)

I

See that ye who call yourselves philosophers
Waver not in the holy cause of truth.
Nay, slay thine own flesh and blood
Rather than sully that holy name.
Neither suppress conviction through fear of misconstruction,
For the Supreme One hateth falsehood and wrong.

II

In many friends there is no real friend;
Let thee and thy friend be one soul in two bodies;
Yet be thoughtful in conduct towards thy friend,
Being ever to him what thou wouldst have him be to thee.

III

In considering the phenomena of nature and doings of Zeus,
First see well that thou understandest all the facts.
It is these, and not thy senses, which alone warrant conclusions,
So see thy *reasonings* as to causes, outstrip them not;
Thy general principles must accord with them—
Rather lag behind than go before them.

IV

Seekest thou my thoughts on hidden things—the unproven?
Know then that thou hast a soul, the light of thy body.
As the sailor lives in and moves the vessel,
So lives thy immortal soul in its mortal tabernacle.
It existed before it, and will exist separate from it;
For it is the eternal eye and ever moving motive force.
Remember also that God gave thee this soul and a free will
In order that morality might be possible to thee.

V

Our God is beyond thought—the *Noésis Nóeseos*—
Thought thinking upon itself—divine and impersonal reason.

VI

Cleanse and purify thy heart, for it is the seat of all sin;
Not by worthless ceremonies, prayers, and moanings,
But by stern resolve to sin no more—to uphold right
And do right. Sacrifice thyself at the shrine of duty;
Forgiving injuries, and acting only towards others
As you would have them behave towards thyself.

VII

Seek for that state of perfectness, or holy purity,
Where virtue struggles no longer, but is the natural
Atmosphere of a perfect or holy life.
He who has to strive against his passions
We call continent, but he is still far from "holiness";
For where strife or pain is, body and soul are "imperfect."
Base desire is in this case only forcibly subjugated,*
And virtue only obtained in spite of a still evil nature.
He only is truly good and noble who chooseth virtue
Simply because it is virtue, and seeketh no reward.

* The great Greek seems here to be quoting the very words of Gotama Buddha, and Alexander and his savans would be sure to hear these at this time in India from the mouths of the Buddhist Srāmans.

PYRRHO

FL. 320 (B.C. 360-270)

I

Have I not seen the wise and studious ones of the East
Believing in many strange creeds and gods? *
In all faiths, their votaries say, there is salvation;
I deny not nor assert. I seek goodness and tranquility.

II

The problems which faiths propose are insoluble to man;
For we have no criterion of absolute truth.
Our knowledge is but knowledge of phenomena,
And phenomena are but the appearances of things.
Now things appear different at different times,
And to different people at the same time.
Silence therefore, rather than dogmatism becometh the wise;
Let him assert nothing, nay nor assert that there is nothing.

III

Yet though thou canst not fathom the deep things of Zeus,
(For creed-makers rush in where angels fear to tread),
And though certain knowledge of the infinite and his creation
Is unattainable to us finite ephemeræ,
Yet not so man's chief end—virtue and duty.

IV

Strive thou therefore after these holy things,
And seek diligently after truth, justice and repose of mind—
An equanimity independent of external circumstances.

* Pyrrho was an artist in the suite of Alexander the Great.

EPIKUROS

fl. 300 b.c. (342-270)

I

Hesiod long ago told us that all from chaos came;
But whence came chaos? I ask, and none reply!
The universe is to me a marvel of order and beauty,
A concourse of atoms, mayhap fortuitously assembled.

II

I say not eat and drink for to-morrow ye die,
Because this is not happiness to a reasonable being.
Let philosophy and reason guide thee to happiness.
Properly considered, it is indeed man's chief end,
Though mere pleasure is not the sovereign good,
Far less carnal or selfish gratifications.

III

Wisely exercise thy reason and control the senses.
What are commonly called the "joys or pleasures of life,"
Are transient and more often evil than wholesome.
Only the ignorant err in hastening after present joys.
Pleasure is purest and most lasting to him who is moderate,
Not to the indulgent votary of ease or voluptuousness.

IV

The philosopher abstains till he knows the end;
Nay, he endures present pain for a future reward,
Equalising rather than intensifying his appetites.
He knows that physical joys compare not with mental,
Hence he seeks for culture in the spiritual or intellectual.

V

The good and virtuous life will be ever the happiest one,
And is the result of knowledge chastened by reason,
That which subordinates self to unselfish conduct.

VI

Contentment is indeed the greatest riches ;
Better few wants than many possessions ;
Though giving one power for good unto others,
They are wasteful of time, and untranquilizing.

VII

Wise men who deny the God of the ignorant masses
Are not profane, nay, rather those who accept him.
For the ignorant neither can know nor understand
A pure God and intellectual heavenly rest.

ZENÖN OF KITION, The Stoik
FL. 260 B.C.

I

God is the universe, nature, law, order and harmony
And this world is but a transitory phase of him.
He is the principle containing and preserving nature,
All the parts of which are but embodiments of him.

II

These manifest his orderly and wise government,
His all-seeing benevolence, power and foreknowledge.
He is the universal force, fire, soul, spirit and law ;
The example after which our souls should follow.

III

If we would obtain peace and unanimity of life,
We must study the constant and serene flow of law,
Harmonizing our lives and wills accordingly,
For only by law is right and goodness accomplished,
And wrong, vice and the vicious restrained.

IV

He who has willed and accomplished virtue
Has attained to the highest moral law;
But every truly moral action is as virtuous as another,
If it spring from our volitions guided by right reason.
It is then consistent with nature, the soul and truth,
And the renunciation or opposite of this is vice.

V

That which is merely fit and proper has no real moral value,
For though good, goodness was not the aim or intention.
The will must be free, and our soul must love virtue,
If we would be like nature's universal spirit.

VI

A passive condition, neither willed nor reasoned out,
Is an unmoral state, and e'en leads to immorality.
Evil must be not only uprooted by reason,
But it must be replaced by knowledge and goodness.

VII

The seat of the affections and sensations is the soul;
It receives from these impressions and knowledge
Or consciousness, and becomes that inward monitor
And guide which is called the conscience.

VIII

But we require experience to avoid its deceptions,
And pureness of heart to attain happiness;
Though happiness must not be our sole aim in life,
For this would be self-seeking, and may make good evil.

IX

Our natural wants necessarily control us,
As do also the habits, laws and customs of our fellows;
And as these work together for good and help the weakly,
They should be respected and never lightly cast aside.

X

The immutable laws of *All-Existent Matter*
Circumscribe and limit us on every side,
And though perchance controlled by heaven,
They are to us supreme, boundless, and eternal.

N.B.—Zenōn was a Buddhistically inclined Stoik who corresponded with Asôka, the Jaino-Buddhist Emperor of Māgadha.

KLÉANTHÉS

FL. 250 B.C.

I

"Greatest of Gods, far-famed, Almighty Zeus,
Author of Nature, arbiter of fate,
All hail! It's fitting that the mortal race
Should call on thee. . . . . . .
Without thine aid, O Zeus, no work is done
In earth or sea, or heaven's ethereal space,
Save what the wicked in their folly do.

II

Thou bringest order from confusion forth,
And jarring discords blend in harmony.
For thou hast so combined the good and ill
In nice adjustment, that in Nature's plan
Eternal reason all pervading reigns.
But for this rule, the wicked would escape.

III

Do thou, O Sire, of every gift, Dispenser,
Lord of the thunder, cloud-pavillion'd Zeus,
Save us from stupid ignorance and folly,
Disperse the brooding darkness from our souls." *

IV

As our master Zeus taught, the soul is immortal
And will receive a place according to its worth;
Until then, strive thou against every passion,
For he who yields to joy must also suffer grief.
As all things are governed by unavoidable necessity,
The wise stoic submits and complains not.

KELTIK OR DRUIDIK TEACHING

OF ABOUT 1ST CENT. B.C.

I

Trust in the Almighty, He will not deceive thee,
He giveth prosperity to the good and those who importune Him;
But not even He can procure good for the wicked,
Nor prosperity for him who is not industrious.

* Mr W. H. Allen's rendering of what he calls "the noblest Theistic poem ever written."

II

All things endure only for a season,
And persevering patience will overcome affliction ;
The virtuous and the happy are of equal age,
And prosperity is often the outcome of adversity.

III

Have patience, it is man's fairest light,
And in thy trouble be not allured to vice.
The thief loveth darkness, the good man light,
But no man can eventually thrive by vice.

IV

Happy is the guileless one who is patient,
And the discreet, who associate not with fools.
After arrogance comes abasement,
But shame has no place on the cheek of the upright

V

Penury bringeth anxiety in its train,
Yet real desolation only reaches the unjust.
Give less heed to thine ear than to the eye,
Nor obstruct the future to provide for the present.

VI

To deceive the innocent is wickedly disgraceful,
And the most painful of diseases is that of the heart.
A useful calling is more valuable than a treasure,
And maidenly modesty than fine apparel.

VII

Like a ship without sail, anchor or rudder,
Is the man who despises advice ;
And woe to that land where there is no religion.

LUCRETIUS CARUS

FL. 50 B.C. (95/9-55/1)

I

Forbear thy crude superstitions and study MATTER.
Know and rely upon her LAWS; they govern all things,
And *Ex nihilo nihil fit*; that which is once begotten
Can never be recalled into nothingness.

II

The beginning of all things are Atoms, which are
Eternally moving through space, forming, separating,
And re-forming in endless variety and potentiality;
But ever according to affinities governed by fixed Laws.

III

MATTER is indivisible down to its ultimate atoms,
Strong in their unity and imperishable substratum.
These require only time—mayhap ages—and circumstances,
To render all combinations and creations possible;
But no supernatural agencies, Spirits or Intelligences,
Only fixed Laws, which produce each its own spontaneously.

IV

MATTER is everywhere, and always full of *Force*, *Life*,
Or *Activity*, though we speak of it as latent.
Mind, as well as body is one of its developments,
And in the complex neurotik and cerebral tissues,
It gives to us our souls, consciousness and memory.

V

The Universe " the ALL, consists of *body* and of *space*,
This moves, and that affords the *motion* place;
But some dull souls think matter cannot move
Into fit shapes without the powers above,
And therefore fancy that the gods did make
And rule this *All*. How great is that mistake.
'Tis death alone dissolves and breaks the chain,
Scattering all things to their first seeds again.
'Tis plain that souls and minds are born and grow,
And all by age or accident decay as bodies do."

VI

Yet has *Fear*, nay, shuddering awe, covered the
Earth with shrines full of wickedness, foolish rites, and
Superstitions, cruel sacrifices, hatred and a dogmatism
Which ignores the laws governing matter.

CICERO

FL. 45 B.C.

I

The order, beauty and all the phenomena of the universe
Proclaim the existence of a Supreme and Eternal Being.
His powers and activities infinitely surpass ours,
And point to a divine, spiritual and free intelligence—
One apart from the corruptions due to matter and time,
Eternal in its nature, and to us incomprehensible.

II

Every citizen must be taught regarding the gods
That they direct all things by their power and wisdom,
Are kind and benevolent to the good, and just to the wicked,
Can see all secrets and judge the intentions of the heart.

III

The gods are not the authors of what we call evil,
Even death is a necessity—the rest and refuge of all.
Nought is chance, but all has been foreseen by Jove,
And he makes the hereafter difficult only to the wicked.

IV

Pray to Jove for all things external and beyond thee,
As for a good climate and against plagues and enemies,
But seek not for that which thine own efforts can accomplish,
As contentment, courage, and victory over evil.

HILLEL, JEWISH HIGH PRIEST
FL. 30 B.C.

I

Do unto others as thou wouldst be done by,
And whatsoever thou wouldst not others should
Do unto thee, do not thou to thy fellows—
This is the substance of the law and the prophets,
All the rest is but commentary thereon.

II

The true Pharisee is he who, from love to the Father,
Doeth his will honestly and with his whole heart.

III

A name magnified is a name destroyed
For the humble man shall be exalted
And the proud man humbled.

IV

Greatness flies if pursued, and follows him who runs.
Be thou diligent for thy day is short,
And say not thou wilt study when leisure comes,
For it never cometh to the procrastinator.

V

He who learns not, or diverts the law to his own good,
Is not worthy of life; he diminishes learning,
Like as all do who increase it not, for Yahve only
Helps the diligent—those striving after truth and right.

VI

Every sin yielded to will be thorns in thy path,
Disabling thee from comprehending the noble and true.

VII

Righteousness is peace, and vulgarity is not piety;
Neither associate with, nor live near, a pious fool.

VIII

Where there are no men, endeavour thou to be a man,
And know that a good name is better than a king's crown;
And that better is the diligent worker than he who fears God.
He fills the universe as does the soul the body;
Yet, like Him, it is not seen, though seeing all.

IX

Let thy good works be considered higher than all thy learning,
And judge not thy neighbor till thou be in his place.

X

This world is a roadside inn; beyond lies thy eternal home.
The righteous man is therefore a striver after goodness,
Knowing no rest either in this world or mayhap in the next.

XI

The strong man is he who can control himself;
The rich man he who is satisfied with his lot.
Wisdom is his who is quick to hear and slow to forget,
And the reverse of this is an evil lot.

XII

If thy wife be small, bend lowly and whisper to her,
Let her heart be thy sanctuary, her presence thy home;
For know, that the blessed union of man and woman
Is the radiance of heaven's Shekinah on earth.

PHILO JUDÆUS

FL. 20 A.C. (20 B.C.—50 A.C.)

I

Yahve spake to man in times past in allegories,
That seeing they might see, but only the wise understand,
Lest his mysteries be trampled under foot by the
Ignorant, and in his wrath he consume them.

II

The mysteries of our Genesis, its patriarchs and leaders,
Are allegories of too deep significance for the uninitiated.

III

Nothing can be generated out of nothing, so neither can anything
Which exists be destroyed, so as to become non-existent,
How could any thing be generated out of that which exists not?

IV

Study the Law—the school-master and guide of the good,
So that thy daily conduct be approved by God and man;
For the Creator is the Law-maker, Law-giver and Father—
Our God the absolutely perfect but incomprehensible *Ālĕ-im*.

V

He changes not nor combines with matter or spirit,
But is "The Eternal One," exalted "above all predicates."
Even thy thoughts cannot reach unto him;
Only by his phenomena canst thou know him.

VI

The beautifully formed universe proclaims him
As "Al-Shadi, the wise and intelligent first cause"
Whom to try and know, contemplate and communicate with,
Should be the ultimate object and joy of his creatures.

VII

He sent his Logos to mediate with a world lying in wickedness;
For the "Absolutely Perfect," Infinite and Immutable,
Could not dwell with the imperfect and changeable;
So "The Word" became "The Fashioner" and Judging Spirit,
The power, the speech, the wisdom of the eternal,
Incarnating the spiritual, invisible and incomparably divine.

VIII

Yahvê acted on primeval, lifeless and quiescent matter,
Conceived, divided and arranged the unformed, which was
Potential of evil and imperfection like to our own carnality,
And which resisted and resists the divine influence.

IX

The Logos is the effulgence of the Father's glory,
A primal existence of pure light around His throne,
Separated from which we are in Kimmerian darkness,
Deepening in intensity the further we recede therefrom.

SENECA

FL. 40 A.C. (10 B.C. TO 65 A.C.)

This learned tutor of the Emperor Nero was an eklektik Stoik and sincere Theist. Though living in the centre of an impure and corrupt court and capital, he has handed down to us some of the highest, truest and most practical ethikal teaching; so much so that he has been claimed as a Christian, and even a teacher of Paul, in fourteen letters to that apostle; and certainly Paul's *quasi* writings, as they appeared long after Seneca's death, are in substance, and often even in words, those of the great Roman. It is of course highly improbable that Seneca, a wealthy noble and, after the royal families, perhaps the second person in the Empire, ever heard of and far less corresponded with the poor itinerant preacher; but it is almost a certainty that all the world knew the religious teaching of the great noble, more especially Paul, who is believed to have been in Rome when Seneca was the most prominent person in the Empire.

I

God is ever present with us, nay within us;
He has a fatherly mind; loves and cherishes the good;
Exercises his providence and power over all men and things,
And without God, no man can be upright and good.

II

He listens to our prayers, and in mercy pardons men's errors,
And heeds not the reproaches of the ignorant and ungodly.
Imitate then thy God, who is good even to the ungrateful,
Giving sunshine and rain alike to good and bad,
And leaving the seas open even to pirates.

III

God's supreme intelligence fashioned the world,
Providing for the needs of all men and creatures,
And it is he who sustains and governs all things.
He subjected all animals and things to man,
And endowed him with a mind swifter
And more searching than the winds of heaven,
Anticipating the stars and planets in their courses,
And enabling him to subdue nature to his purposes.

IV

What is Nature but God? presiding over Reason,
And penetrating through all parts of the wondrous whole,
Tempering the seasons for man's varied needs,
And anticipating and over-ruling all for his use.

V

Yet Jove's ways are secret and past finding out,
For "he encloses himself within himself,"
And our vision reaches only to part of his works.
Of matter *per se* we are ignorant, seeing only phenomena;
But our thoughts can dwell upon his attributes,
And our daily lives make manifest our adoration.

VI

He has placed "within us his own *sacer spiritus*,"
To guide and aid us in discerning good from evil;
For "sinful we have been, are, and will be;"
Yet conscience can hold up heaven's mirror,
Rebuke and recall us, if it be not seared or sullied
By repeated neglects of the divine voice.

VII

Let the acquisition of wisdom be the purpose of thy life,
Which "is not really short unless thou make it so."
Be brave and good, overcoming thine inate failings.
Neither be appalled by dangers, cast down by adversity,
Nor elated by praise and prosperity, but maintain
A spirit of impassiveness and gentle equanimity.

VIII

To be happy we must court neither power nor wealth,
For both are snares, and usually prove enemies
To the acquisition of knowledge and virtue.
To be truly virtuous requires much wisdom,
Which few have leisure or can attain unto.
Yet "let not learning be bound by thy necessities,
For this is intemperance" akin to pride and self-seeking.

IX

Learn from Epikuros that "the knowledge of sin
Is the first necessary step towards regeneration";
Therefore keenly review thy words and deeds, neither
Omitting, excusing nor hiding aught from thyself.
Fear not to cast out from thy heart, mind or life,
All that has led or prompted to evil; yea, if
Need be, pluck out the offending member itself.

X

The divine sower cast abroad good seed, but some
Fell on barren marshy ground, and other from
Neglect produces only thorns and weeds, not grain.
See thou prove the wise and good husbandman,
For fruits correspond with the seed sown, and the
Produce, with the intelligence and care bestowed.

XI

Good cometh not from evil, nor figs from the olive tree;
Nor from an unclean vessel, however bright outside,
Can flow pure water; so from an evil heart can
Only come evil thoughts—maturing wicked deeds.

XII

Embark not on distant hopes; saying I will buy,
Build, acquire wealth and honors, and rest sated;
Alas, we know not what the morrow may bring forth;
And happiness depends not on these, but on a good life.

XIII

Virtue calleth unto us and "is barred unto none,
Inviting kings and gentlefolks, bond and free," and saying:
"Wheresoever man is, there is room for doing good."

XIV

The good ones must toil, spend and be spent for mankind.
Live for others and not self, for a cross, rather than a crown.
Better virtue and peace of mind than royal honors
And the palm branch, with an eager, aching heart.

XV

Thy duties to others are imperative, and should be hearty,
Agreeable and gentle, this even to the churlish.
To enemies be yielding and at all times just.
Be slow to "mark the pimples upon others,
And keenly remember the ulcers on thine own body."

PERSIUS, ROMAN STOIK AND POET
34 TO 62 A.C.

"Let us present a sacrifice to heaven
Dearer than tribes by graceless greatness given;
Composed affections, thoughts from malice free,
A heart deep tinctured with humanity;
Such is the sacrifice the gods demand;
A cake suffices from a spotless hand."

EPICTETUS
80 A.C.

I

Love not darkness nor shut the door of thy mind
To light or argument, however little thou likest them;
For this is to reject the deity and thy divine part or *daimon*—
That inner prophet, conscience, never resting,
Divine and incorruptible guardian, without
Which thou canst not know good from evil.

II

Jove requires thee to be faithful to every truth
And true to every fresh light he sendeth thee;
Yea, that thou shouldst accept it though thou suffer for it.
Be faithful to him even unto death.
Pray to him as an ever-present introspector,
And let thy communings be frequent.
Accept his decrees with a contented spirit.

III

Let goodness be thy aim, not avarice or self-seeking.
Even learning will not protect thee from these;
Nor can learning alone, purify thy moral nature.
This is the highest and best result of true philosophy;
It should teach us to resist evil and love goodness,
And give us even in want and sorrow contented minds.

IV

Rest not on any mere theory, "prating only to others,"
Practise the virtues thou knowest, and control even thy conceptions.

V

That only is good or evil which we are free to choose.
Nothing external to man controls his choice;
Not even Jove, but reason which makes us superior to brutes.
Whoso repudiates reason, falls from the divine;
For the essence of deity is Reason, Mind and Knowledge—
The trinity of nature, a completeness which pleaseth God.

VI

The essence of true religion is purity and goodness,
The abstaining from evil, however much we suffer;
Bearing all things that we may accomplish good.

VII
He doeth well even though he forsake wife and family,
So that he may more perfectly serve Jove and man,
Live more for others and less unto himself.

THE EMPEROR M. AURELIUS ANTONINUS
Fl. 160 (121-180) A.C.

I
Thou canst not separate the past from the present
Any more than dissever nature's rigid continuity.
Law rules all in just sequence—foreseeable by the wise,
And ordained by the deity for the righteous rule of the whole.

II
Be content though evil happen unto thee,
Yea though the universe appear an ungoverned chaos—
A wild torrent without a path or purpose,
For only through ills and suffering does man progress.

III
Act well thy part, but let reason govern thee;
Neither fear nor flatter, and seek wisdom from the gods
For they wish thee to be rational like unto themselves.
Ask them to remove from thee unjust fears concerning them,
And to bestow upon thee knowledge of thy real defects.

IV
Let a true philosophy keep thee from pride and selfishness,
Making thee conscious of thy many shortcomings,
And swift to determine what is true in judgments.

V

Be gentle and forgiving, tempering justice with mercy.
Strive to diffuse happiness with a cheerful spirit;
Alleviate, and where possible, raise the condition of all,
Of women, children, slaves and others within thy influence,
Be the help of the destitute and physician to the sick,
Honor all as if brethren, then will mutual love abound.

VI

The precepts of the Law form a Religion of charity and justice;
Giving all their dues, and helping them to live righteously.
If thou canst say: " I have not spoken or acted wrongly,"
Then indeed hast thou well fulfilled thy part.

VII

Humanity apart from the gods requires thee to forgive injuries;
To show no wrath nor return evil for evil;
Nay, abstain even from the thought of evil, and so fashion
Thy soul as much as may be into the divine likeness.

VIII

Let " right reason, the *Orthos Logos*, as a divine emanation,"
Be thy guide, and duty—pleasant or irksome—thy manly religion.
Cultivate that *Logos* or divine spirit which is within thee
By a life of lofty moral purity, unstained by hope of benefits,
Then shalt thou understand the Logos which unites thee with divinity.
He sins who tries " to bargain with the silent infinite " for reward.
Expect nought, be righteous and fear not thy end, for he
Is but half a man who disquiets himself as to death.

IX

It is not enough to do good ; do it for its own sake,
Without a thought of benefit or even gratitude in return ;
And " whisper it not to another, but pass on to fresh deeds,"
Even as the vine produces its fruits, still pressing upwards.

X

Many grains of incense burn on the same altar ;
What matters it if one drops sooner or later into the flame ;
Be ready to yield up life like the ripe olive ; blessing the
Earth nurse, and thanking the mother tree which bore us.

Gleanings from TURANIAN or PRE-ARYAN INDIANS
Usually called "Aborigines," of whom there are 40,000,000.

SONTÂLS OF SOUTHERN BANGÂL HILLY TRACTS,
A RACE OF GREAT ANTIQUITY.

I

We simple ones love justice and fear and resist coercion ;
But will fly our beloved land to live in peace.

II

Great crimes are unknown amongst us ;
And we have no laws relating unto criminals.

III

Of hard and uncharitable men we know many.
They will be sufferers both now and hereafter ;
Also they who try to make money of the stranger,
And feel no pain in the distress of another.

IV

Man must live chastely and be the husband of one wife
Content with what heaven bestows, and loving all.

BODDOS AND DHIMALS OF EASTERN INDIA

I
Have no dealings with the violent. War is unnecessary :
Live in peace with all, especially neighboring peoples.

II
Excel in honesty and strive to live well thine own life,
Yet cringe not before the wayward and covetous.
Be firm and truthful, amicable and charitable,
Offering hospitality freely unto all men.

III
Be chaste, and despise unchastity and divorce,
Loving thy wife and keeping her only unto thee.
Treat her with respect, confidence and kindness,
And let her not labor outside thine own house.
Love, protect and respect thy children,
Teaching them kind and peaceful ways.

LEPCHAS, KUCHES and HÓS. of N.E. India

I
See thou be truthful in all matters,
Yea, tho' a lie might save thy life.

II
Be the husband of one wife, and be true to her
As thou desirest she may be to thee.

III
Be affable and kind, desiring rather to give than receive.
Excel in honesty and in the forgiveness of injuries,
Making up differences by generous concessions ;
So that mutual respect, not malice, abound.

ARAFURAS AND JAKUNS. (Trans-India)

I

Let us have brotherly love and live at peace,
Seeking wealth and power only to alleviate misery.

II

Askest thou "if I have a soul and have heard of a future state?"
Verily the Arafura knoweth not such matters.
None have returned to us after death,
How, then, can such things be learned?
"Who created this world and all in and around it?"
Truly we knew not that it had been created.
Many have spoken to us about these things,
But none have said anything reliable.
When we die, the wise say there is an end of us.

To this very much might be added. In Mr Lyall's *Ind. Poems* a wild Indian aborigine replies as follows to the above cross-questioning of a missionary:—

"Thou sayest I have a soul, a spirit that never dies:
If He was content when I was not, why not when I pass by?"

POLYNESIANS, TONGANS, AND ADJACENT ISLANDERS.
THEIR VERY ANCIENT TEACHINGS.

I

Be ye kind one to another;
True and faithful to all thy brethren,
And especially to those of thine own house.

II

Honour thy father and thy mother,
Treating them tenderly and thoughtfully;
Nor fail to be respectful and helpful to the aged.

III

Have too much respect for thyself to steal,
Or even to covet that which is thy neighbour's.

IV

Be not a tale-bearer nor slanderer,
And abhor blasphemy and all irreligion.

V

Chastity and a good name is woman's crown and glory,
And should also be that of every self-respecting man.

VI

Practise hospitality, not only to the stranger but to all,
And let none say of thee: "He is selfish and uncharitable.

VII

Strive to act and speak nobly and generously,
Not from fear of misfortunes here and hereafter,
But for the inward happiness and peace which
Goodness confers on the good and just man.*

AZTEKS, OF OUR MIDDLE AGES

Keep peace with all men, thine own nation
No less than the stranger tribes around thee.
Art thou injured, wait patiently and be humble;
For the Supreme One sees and will right thee.
Be chaste, nay look not curiously on any woman,
For this is to commit sin with thine eyes.

* A great deal of similar moral and pious teaching will be found in early writings of Polynesian missionaries, as in *Mariner*, &c., and see Prof. Huxley in *Nineteenth Century Review*, Ap. 1886.

PORPHYRIOS

FL. 295 A.C. (233-205)

I

Our God is not all things, nor divided among all,
Yet is in all things, and present everywhere.
He containeth all, and is yet separate and apart from all,
He is the source of all multitude, yet a perfect unity.

II

He is present totally to every worshipper as a God,
Intellect and soul.   Being everywhere he is nowhere.
As all-pervading intellect, he is in no subordinate essences,
But as intellect he possesses the soul, which is everywhere,
Though in respect to body nowhere.
Yet body exists in soul, intellect and God,
And the intellect is the cause of souls.

III

Seek the Supreme, and wrestle with him in prayer,
For this conjoins the good man with divinity;
But animadvert not on heaven, nor pray for worldly benefits,
Strive rather to elevate thy soul and dispose it
For the reception of supreme illumination.
As heated paper when placed near the flame
Becomes wrapped in the divine element,
So strive to get heated in thy devotions,
That thou mayest readily burst into flame.

From the transcendental vagaries of Porphyry may have sprung many of the Christian extravagances of the monks and priests of our Middle Ages. The Athanasian creed of the sixth century looks like a direct evolution of some of his mystical teaching.

MAHAMAD, The Arabian Prophet
fl. 600 a.c. (570-632)

This great "Messenger of Āllah" taught as follows in the *Korān* and some authoritative discourses.

I
Allah is Light, the brightness of heaven and earth;
The Light of Lights, who giveth only according to his will.
He is a light unto those who seek him; ever dwelling
In the chamber of his saints, and making bright their
Morning and evening sacrifice of prayer and praise.

II
It is he who giveth daylight and darkness, heat and cold;
He gathers together and disperses the clouds of heaven,
Sending sunshine and rain unto whom he pleases
And withholding it from others as he deems fit.
Who art thou to question the Creator and Giver?

III
Whom he willeth, he saves, therefore pray thou without ceasing.
To whom he giveth no light, there is no light;
Thou canst not even intercede with Allah till
He so guide thy will—an act of his good pleasure.
Salvation is purely a gift of his free grace.

IV
Out of nothing and for his own purpose, he created all,
And whom he created, he also predestinated;
Knowing and ordering everything from the beginning.
Therefore is he the author of evil as well as good;
Of war, pestilence and famine, of hell as well as heaven.

V

He loveth Islām, imposing "mercy on himself":
And his children in paradise will gaze "with scorn"
On the everlasting torments of the damned.
Fear him if so be thou wouldst be saved,
And listen unto the teaching of his "messenger";
For he standeth by the portals of the heavens,
And without him none may enter therein.

VI

Though thy path be dark and thorny, still trust ĀLLĀH;
He dealeth ever righteously, if inscrutably,
Rewarding all, high and low, according to their faith,
To some he giveth even now, but to all hereafter.

VII

He sees thee when none observe, and accepts the secret
Aspirations of the heart as well as of the lips.
Seek communion therefore with him at all times
And places—amidst the stated assemblies of his people,
As well as at those others he specially prescribes.
Seek him austerely in the annual fasts and *Hāj;*
Performing every rite and ceremony prescribed for
The faithful at the sacred seasons and shrines.

VIII

"When thou prayest, turn towards the holy place"
And to "Safa and Marwa—the beacons of God."
Neglect them not; it is good to make pilgrimages there,
And to circumambulate the *K'aba* with prayers and praise.
It is the special chosen place of the Ruler of heaven and earth,
Who wearieth not, nor is perplexed by the burden
Of things, nor by the worship of his people.

IX

All in the heavens and earth worship ÁLLĀH;
But worship thou him *only*—not the orbs which
He has created—sun, moon or the elements.
He is "the only ever living and self-subsistent One;
The brightness of eternity and the lamp of truth";
And only in communion with him cometh light,
Else is life a vain show—frivolous and unprofitable.

X

Neglect no ordinance of thy tribe nor duty of thy station;
Remember that he who obeys a good impulse, to him
It is good, and "Āllāh knoweth it, and is grateful."
Observe every good and moral law of man
For the Lord's sake, thy fellows, and thine own profit,
And as an example for thy children to do likewise.

XI

Honor thy spiritual rulers, temporal though they be;
Also kings and chiefs, for their authority is from God.

XII

Fight only in the armies of Allah and slay the seditious,
But be merciful when they desist, and pardon the penitent,
And if thou canst, release the captives.

XIII

Allah is no respecter of persons or of nations,
Punishing all who sin, be they high or low—even
Islāmis and the pious, each according to their deeds and faith.
Whoso among the faithful publicly confesseth their faults
Will not perish overlastingly like the infidel race.

XIV

Seek justice for thy kindred, more especially for Islam ;
Turn not the beggar or needy from thy door,
Nor any faithful poor ones from thy midst,
Nor any stranger guest from thy house and board.

XV

Lend to none with usury, nor to thy kinsman with interest,
Nor, till of full age, touch the wealth of the orphan ;
For Allah protects these and all the poor of Islam.

XVI

Health, power and position are gifts lent to thee by God,
And to him thou must render account thereof.
They are plants nourished by his rains, and
Whether corn or stubble, lent to thee for a purpose.
Give therefore offerings of all thou possessest.

XVII

Thou mayest eat all things not forbidden in *Al-Korān*,
But drink no wine nor play games of chance.
If thou canst not pardon a brother, prosecute reasonably,
Causing him kindly to do that which is just ;
For evil is best repelled by goodness and justice.

XVIII

Let thine own and thy wife's raiment be simple,
And her adorning be only unto her lord.
Rule well and wisely thine own house and affairs,
Exercizing economy and avoiding excess,
And where possible all appearance of rule.

XIX

Alike in home, camp and council, acknowledge God;
And be bold in confessing him and all truths,
Nor shrink from enforcing and acting upon the same.
Slur not over any commandments of Allah,
And be forward to announce his attributes.

XX

Praise him, frequently and openly, crying aloud
That " He only is God—The One, and Mahamad his prophet";
That " He is the only ruler, guide and judge of living and dead,
Knowing all that is and shall be—The Everlasting,
The Unbegotten and Unbegetting, Omnipotent and Omniscient—
The One without a second, compeer or comparison—
A Being, personal yet incorporeal and incomprehensible."

XXI

Presume not to speak, nay *think*, of three Gods,
Nor of " three in one," nor of a Messiah-God;
Nor compare to Allah, " Jesus the Nazarine, son of Mary,"
Nor Abraham, Moses or other servant of " The Eternal."

XXII

Honor and invoke him as " the one and only eternal Father-God,"
And serve and love him, his archangels, angels and all
The " Company of the Faithful," here and hereafter.
Frequently contemplate the resurrection of saints,
The passage before the judgment seat, and a life for ever
With Allah, and the spirits of the just made perfect.

XXIII

None indeed who deny Allah and his prophet can be saved,
But to Sabean, Jew and Christian, or those who of ignorance
Know not Islam, "there need come no fear,
Neither shall they grieve "—God is Merciful.

N.B.—The above are but a few of the leading teachings of this great Arabian, as found in the Korān and his best recognised discourses, but his history, bible, and the religions of Arabia, before and during his time, will be found carefully epitomised in our *Short Studies*.

PRINTED BY
TURNBULL AND SPEARS
EDINBURGH

www.ingramcontent.com/pod-product-compliance
Lightning Source LLC
Chambersburg PA
CBHW021937160426
43195CB00011B/1119